HOOKED

Cindy,
We hope you enjoyed the story!

Hooked

Lessons of the Heart From a Little Horse in Cabo

Christie Bonham

Disclaimer

This book is a work of creative nonfiction. I have recreated the events, locations and conversations from my memories of them. While all the stories are true, I have changes some names and identifying characteristics to protect the privacy of the people involved. Some of the events have been compressed to best represent the essence of the story. Word for word transcript of actual conversations is not presented here nor do I pretend to believe I could remember them word for word. Rather the truth as best as I can recall.

———

ISBNs: 978-1-7334513-0-7 (paperback); 978-1-7334513-3-8 (hardcover); 978-1-7334513-1-4 (ePub); 978-1-7334513-2-1 (Kindle)

Library of Congress Catalog Number: 2019912169
Printed in the United States of America
First Printing: 2019
23 22 21 20 19   5 4 3 2 1

Cover photograph by Denise Green
Book design by Mayfly Design

Milagro Publishing
P.O. Box 982855
Park City, UT 84098

To order, visit christielbonham.com

For Keith and Milagro

If light is in your heart, you will find your way home.

—RUMI

Contents

Acknowledgments

WRITING THIS BOOK HAS BEEN cathartic in ways I could not have imagined. It has been both hard and rewarding at the same time. I am so thankful for my husband, Keith, who not only joined in the quest to give Milagro a family of his own but has long been a voice of encouragement for me to tell this story. His belief in my writing gave me the courage to step out and do something I'd never dreamed possible. Thank you for having faith in me and for giving me the space to think and to dream. Without that, I could never have completed this book.

I am eternally grateful for my cousin Katrina, who spent days and nights with me in our youth, riding the hills of California on our ponies. Without these moments I would never have horses in my heart the way I do today. Your friendship and the mutual bond we share has been and will forever be treasured.

For the people of Cabo who took Milagro in when he was at the end of his rope, Elizabeth and Saul, who gave him a place to mend his broken body and trust again, along with Fran and Linda, who allowed me into their place of sanctuary so that I could also heal and grow; thank you.

To my longtime friend Donna Ryan, who, once she heard the story, told me I just had to write this book, your enthusiasm and support have been there to cheer me on in this lengthy process. Thank you for believing in me and for seeing the true beauty of this story.

To my family and friends, my brother Tony, sister-in-law Cindy, brother Mike, and sister-in-law Vicki, being able to share this project and my excitement with you has meant more to me than you would know. Just the support of the people who mean the most has been so special.

To my editor, Audra, of Creative Detail: thank you for your kind and thoughtful guidance in polishing this book. You have a special ability to probe gently and bring out the essence and truth of a story. I am grateful to have found you, and for your steadfast dedication and professionalism.

To my proofread editor, Annie Harvieux: you took the book and elevated it to a new level with your keen eye and unique editorial style. You brought a fresh read to this story and helped it shine.

For Milagro, the horse who started it all by filling in the blanks of my life and putting me back on the right path. There simply are no words to describe what you mean to me. I only hope that by me sharing this story, others will know you and see the greatness in you. I hope they will understand the sense of destiny and the eternal bond we share. There is no greater gift than you.

And for Mom and Dad, you saw a spark in your little girl that needed to be fed, and you gave your precious time and valuable resources because you understood it made me feel complete. Your love and friendship are cherished and missed, and an important part of my life today and always. If not in body, in spirit, you were with me every step of the way.

Preface

HE WAS BORN IN THE SUMMER, in the early nineties, the son of a hardworking mother and father who had been part of this land for generations. Their blood ran through the *arroyos* that gave shape to this seaside town. Year after year, generation after generation, Spanish horses crossed this desert with the Spanish conquistadors. Descendants of the horses brought to the Americas to conquer this new world, these strong survivors adapted and then flourished as they grew into the desertscape.

A family's heritage runs deep here, deep as the ocean blue. A true historic fixture to the landscape, the horses in these parts are proud. And just as many other families had claimed this slice of the world as their own, Milagro's did so as well.

Milagro entered into this special world under the most difficult of circumstances. A hurricane loomed over the ocean to the south. The sky turned black, and a large wall of dangerous clouds threatened offshore. The wind began to whip, and the rain came down in blasting sheets. A pregnant mare and her herd were shuffled out of their corrals, out past the ranch, and into the open desert. The men who looked after them knew this was their best chance for survival. It was not the first and would not be the last of storms like this. And just like their forefathers, they knew this was now their duty. Leaving the herd in the confines of the corrals could mean certain death. If the waters rose and flooded the corrals, they stood no chance. But the horses knew that they must uphold their responsibility and find shelter in the vast openness of this land to survive the night.

The wind continued to blow fiercely. The trees the horses had taken shelter under swayed. But these trees' roots ran long and strong. They would bend but would not break.

The horses moved in and out of the defensive line to take turns sheltering one another, but the pregnant mare stayed centered inside the protection of her herd. She was beginning to feel the labor pains, and as best she could, she stayed calm.

And then she knew. She lay down on the sand, as it was her only choice. Mother Nature has a way of her own, and as this horrendous hurricane moved over the desert, the mare's body was about to give birth. The familiar pains could no longer be ignored.

Morning broke. The townspeople slowly emerged to find tremendous devastation. Power lines were tossed about like spaghetti, and the roads were covered with debris. An eerie quiet had taken over the town cut off from power.

The men slowly made their way to the *arroyos*, looking for the herd. A few horses had stayed near the barn and were quickly saddled to go search for the others. Scattered about like so much of the debris were some of the herd. A group of three stood on the newly formed beach that had emerged from the storm. Next to them was the carcass of a cow who had not been so lucky. And farther down were cars that had been pushed and tossed like rubber boats and finally landed—buried in the sand at the edge of what was once a beautiful tropical dream, now turned upside down and brown with fury from the waves and wind. The casualties were visible everywhere.

The day passed slowly for the weary mare and her foal, and as the sun began to set, they were finally discovered. The men, exhausted by the sleepless night, had continued to round up the sprawling herd, and just as they began to give up, they saw them. Under the strong limbs of the battered Palo de Arco were the mare and her foal: a chestnut with two white socks on his back legs and a fishhook white blaze on his face. He stood beside his weary mother, wondering what kind of world he had entered into.

The men were shocked and astonished at what they saw. This was one special foal. He had survived the night and had not separated from his mother. How could he be so strong? The thought of this gave them a renewed strength. At a moment when they were at their weakest, this foal came and lifted them all up. And for this, they named him Milagro, which means "miracle."

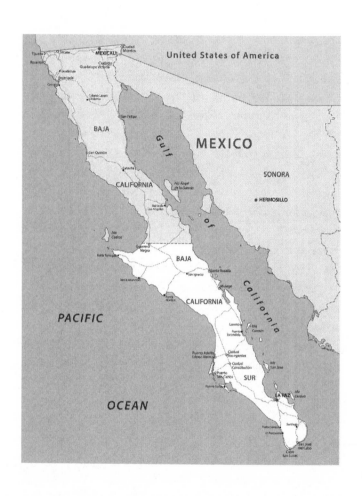

Cabo

As we touched down at the airport in San José del Cabo, the blood rushed back into my head. I felt as though I'd been holding my breath for an eternity, and now it was time to breathe. My husband, Keith, and I were not alone on this flight, as we'd been many times before. Today our yellow Labrador, Roy, and our cat, Kitty, were onboard with us. Today's flight would not be a quick turnaround, as we'd always done in the past. No, today's flight was a one-way trip and the beginning of our life south of the border.

The Great Recession, as it has come to be known, was in full swing. The housing crisis and stock market crash had been slow to cross the border. But as a shattered glass cannot be contained, neither could the economic collapse. In time, it crept slowly and methodically across all borders. And like so many tourists who planned to stay for only a short time, the recession had decided to stick around too. It had come to Cabo and decided to pull up a seat and stay awhile.

Keith was an air-conditioning contractor. After selling his business back in the States, he had moved to Cabo to start a new life. Many years later, he had a thriving business. He had a great team in Cabo. We had been living in Utah and he was commuting back and forth to run his business. But the financial wildfire that had blazed

1

across the United States sent embers over the border, and it eventually took its toll. His short, consistent trips had grown into weeks of triage. The numbers were in, and the books didn't lie—the company was in trouble. There was no way to stop the bleeding from the US. And after many talks and discussions, the choice was clear. He booked a month-long trip to Cabo to find us a place to live. I stayed behind to find tenants for our home and pack us up for a new adventure. A new life was about to unfold.

For Keith, who had lived in Cabo for many years prior, this seemed like more of an inconvenience than a major life change. He'd been an air-conditioning contractor for over thirty years, so he'd put in his time. The plan to slowly back away from the company and allow the employees to buy him out was now on ice. It was all about business for him.

I had a completely different feeling about this new direction. Moving from the mountain town that I had recently grown to love to the unknown of a foreign country scared the shit out of me. I had been to Cabo on many trips, but I had come as a tourist and for short bursts of time. There had always been a beginning, a middle, and an end to our trips down south. Now I was facing a future that was completely unclear and unknown.

The first several months in Cabo were difficult. Keith was suddenly void from my daily peripheral, as he was busy rebuilding his company. I struggled to find meaningful things to fill my time. While my friends back home were busy building careers and raising families, I felt utterly lost. The separation and sense of isolation were more than I had anticipated. We had given up our US cell phones and replaced them with an international substitute. This made me feel even more cut off from the rest of my world. Friends and family had a hard time navigating the international numbers, and as their busy lives moved on in full motion, I felt suspended in time. My phone never rang, or beeped. It was a silent flatline.

And the more time that went quietly by, the more concerned I became about how this whole event was going to unravel. I'd had times in my life when I needed to dig deep and keep the faith. But this time was different. It became more and more apparent that this was something I didn't feel equipped to handle. I was not as strong as I'd once been. I didn't know where my energy and positive attitude had gone. And even scarier to me was not that I had lost them but that I had absolutely no idea where to go looking for them. And I needed to find these missing parts of me. Time was ticking by, and it was imperative that I find something to root me in my new world and bring me around. I was losing myself.

And it wasn't just the change to a new country, but Mexico itself. I had reservations and anxieties about this place that most other newcomers wouldn't. I didn't come here with a blind sense of safety or security, and I had good reason to feel this way.

In high school in the eighties, it had been a pretty common practice for kids to cross the border for fun. The drinking age was seventeen, so many of us ventured down to Tijuana during the summer break from school. Kids from all the high schools went. And on one particular night, I was with a group of friends at the new "fancy" disco. Shortly after arriving, three of us girls went to the bathroom. Two of my friends stayed to touch up makeup or whatnot, so I left to walk back to the table. And that was when I was nearly abducted. The first man who came up to me was dressed in a chicken costume. He told me that I had to leave because I was drunk. Funny, because I hadn't even had a sip of anything to drink. But not so funny was that he wouldn't let me go tell my friends. And as I pleaded with him to let me go tell the group, I was being slowly and methodically herded down a very long hallway with a one-way emergency door at the end. The music was so loud. I couldn't hear myself talk. But in a flash at the end of the hallway, I saw my two friends pass by. And suddenly I screamed. I screamed their names so loudly that they heard me and ran over to me.

Now the second man, dressed in a business suit, was there and neither of them let the girls get to me. So the girls left and ran back to the table, at which point I was finally pushed out the emergency exit. The big door slammed shut. Outside was a loading ramp with a staircase leading down. And down at the bottom of the stairs was a taxi with the lights on and its motor running. The two men were outside with me. I wrapped my arms around the staircase railing and banded them together. The men pulled at me and my legs, tossing my shoes down the stairs. My arms tore up and down the metal railing as they pulled to get me loose. I held on with all my might, knowing that as soon as I let go, I would be shuffled into that taxi and driven off somewhere.

It felt like such a long time, but it must not have been very long at all before the big door swung open and my friends were standing in the doorway. The first person I saw was a friend of mine, a boy who was in our group and went to school with me. He was tall with a solid build and played on our football team. He stood there and demanded to know what was going on. The rest of the group was there, behind him. At that point, the men decided it was no longer worth their fight, so they made us all leave together, out that back exit door, down the stairway, and into the darkness of Tijuana.

We walked until we could summon a taxi to take us back to the border. The taxi that had been waiting with its motor running had suddenly disappeared. Soon we were back in our own car, across the border, and in the safety of our own country. The drive home was utterly silent. Each of us understood what had happened. We all knew that suddenly the reality of this place wasn't what we had thought.

All these years later, that fear would still creep up in me, not only in Mexico but on other occasions as well. But now, living here, I knew I was going to wrestle with it. I would have to come to terms with it. But it was going to take time. And it wasn't that I didn't like Mexico; I just didn't trust it.

The first summer was more of a blur than anything. Keith did his best to show me all the secrets of this new world. On the weekends, we took trips up the coast to secret surf spots where we could sit for hours with only the sparkling Pacific Ocean ahead of us. No people, no footsteps, no interruptions. I practiced yoga and tried to harness a positive attitude. I wrote a journal that scripted some of our experiences. I got to know all the local shopping spots for groceries, and I started to settle. But I found that I was settling for the new me: the girl who had lost her way.

I would look for her in the faces of strangers. People who had just come to town and were here to have a

good time. Smiling, happy, and confident people. People who could calculate each step of each day and know exactly where it was taking them. I felt like walking up to them and starting a conversation so that I could join that world again. I imagined what their lives were like back home and what kind of stories they would share about their Cabo trip. And I envied them. These people, who were like any one person I knew back home, seemed like strange beings that I was able to recognize but was no longer part of their club. And it felt as though they didn't recognize me either. I wanted to scream out.

And then there was Roy—my stable rock, my steady Eddie. Between Keith trying to find a solid landing with his company and me having emotional isolation issues, Roy seemed simply unfazed by our new life. He seemed to flourish. Absolutely all of the fears I had about his health and safety in Mexico had just been fabricated in my mind. The heat didn't bother him. He wasn't mauled and maimed by loose rabid dogs. He wasn't dognapped from our backyard or poisoned because of his barking. He didn't lack social stimulation. All the horrible things I had conjured up in my mind didn't happen.

What did happen, though, was that I leaned on him more than ever. He'd always been steadfast, but he grew tolerant and more careful of my emotions. He knew that I was entrusting him to help me through. Our walks took on a new meaning. Roy and I didn't just walk; we learned to explore. We took chances, and he encouraged me to take one step, and then another. He showed me how to hold my head up high and to smile even though I didn't feel like smiling. Roy lifted up my heart, he opened it, and he sang to it. He sang it a nursery rhyme. He reminded me of all that I kept hidden in my heart. That girl who had been void—that's where she was hiding. She just needed a map showing her how to get back out. Each day, Roy did that for me. He showed me the way back out. He was a companion who never took no for an answer. And with him, I smiled, I laughed, and I grew ever more confident. He led me to the beach and back again. It's amazing how the smallest things can have such significance.

By the time fall rolled around, I began to feel more

like myself again. We had taken a trip to San Diego, and those four days reminded me of my family and friends. I renewed my faith in the process of life and started to feel more positive.

I understood that we were going to be in Cabo for some time to come. And I began to think long and hard about a job or a business that I could do to be productive. I had always worked and contributed. This had been one of the defeating feelings about the move, because the challenges are unique in Mexico. The pay is discouraging at best, and the obstacles in place for foreigners are enough to throw in the towel. But I had landed on a very exciting idea and was eager to tell Keith about it.

Dog Boutique

HAVING OUR DOG, ROY, AND LIVING DOWN SOUTH opened my eyes to some of the shortcomings of Cabo. The place is like an island, so products of any kind are minimal, and it's a challenge to find what you like for yourself, much less for your pet. Roy was on a special diet, which meant we had to order his food online, pay an importation fee, and wait for it to arrive. I figured that others were in the same boat, for finding not only pet food but also all the basics, like quality toys, treats, and even collars and leashes. There was a Costco, where quite a lot of people went to buy dog food, and there were a few veterinarians who sold dusty dog toys that looked as though they had been schlepped down in a suitcase. I was buying products for Roy from the United States and paying the hefty importation fee. What if I could buy items wholesale and offer them in a classy American dog boutique? Would people come? Would they find this interesting? It was early September, and I'd spent the past four months in a funk like no other. This new idea suddenly had me buzzing around with a newfound purpose.

I talked to Keith about it, and he was so supportive. I knew it was asking a lot to take on the opening of a new business, especially in the middle of him trying to right the ship, so to speak, with his company. But Keith was aware of my struggles and knew it was important to have a purpose, so he was behind me all the way. Having him onboard was important. Together we could make this work.

The first step was to secure a *local*—this is what they call commercial space in Cabo. I wanted to have a large presence with the locals. But the town was also centered on tourism. With so many people passing through downtown Cabo on any given day, we needed to draw them in. In our store, they could find gifts for their pets or other pet lovers back home. We had been to a store like the one we envisioned while on a trip in the Caribbean, and it was so fun to stumble upon that boutique. That's what I was shooting for.

I decided to further focus my attention on the cruise-ship crowd. At the time, Cabo had a strong cruise-ship presence, with as many as eighteen ships in a week. They were coming year-round at this time. To have access to a whole new group of cruisers each week made sense. I decided on a *local* that was in the center of the first mall they came across after disembarking from the ships.

We signed the lease, and I came up with the design concept for the store. I wanted a fresh, clean, and uncluttered space that was welcoming and inviting. The store had windows on two walls, which brought in a lot of light. There was a water fountain in the courtyard just outside the front door, and the public restrooms were directly across from the store. The logo I had designed was fun and whimsical. We had the painters use a cool green on the walls, and then we installed dark-brown slat board that made the products pop. And I found fixtures from IKEA that would work.

While the work was being done on the *local*, I spent my days looking up inventory. With Keith's help, I designed a space plan. Then I worked on finding as much unique, fun, and beach- or Cabo-themed merchandise as I could find that would fit into the space. I carefully measured each product to fit into the plan and calculated the cost of importation and shipping to make sure the prices would be attainable. The end result was amazing.

It was now mid-November, and the cruisers were rolling in. High season in Cabo had begun, and each day that went by without being open just killed me. But we waited patiently for all the merchandise to arrive, and soon enough, it did.

We put the store together on November 30. Thanksgiving had passed, and now the time had come. Keith and I spent the day unpacking products. He assembled all the fixtures, and we moved things into just the right places. His technician came by to give the air conditioner a quick tune-up. And by the end of the day, the place was ready to roll. People had already started peeking into the windows and coming in. I even made a few sales that day. Things were looking good for our grand opening.

Cabo Dog

OUR FIRST DAY OF BUSINESS was my birthday, of all days. And we ended up with phenomenal sales. It was a magical moment for me. This store that I had sunk my heart into creating was well received and celebrated by locals and tourists. There were lines of people waiting to make purchases. And my smile just grew as the day went on. It seemed as though all things had suddenly aligned and I was exactly where I was meant to be.

Cabo Dog became a place for me to share with others the love I have always had for animals. It wasn't uncommon for customers to spend an hour or so in this small, cool, and comfortable place. With reggae music playing in the background, they would tell me some of the most amazing stories about their pets back home—some funny, some tender, and occasionally, some deep and emotional. There were the people traveling on cruises, and the local customers were beginning to grow some as well. I had a running advertisement in the local paper. People came looking for treats or a new collar or a leash. Or they just came to shop, to see what this store was all about.

I first met some of the ladies of the Los Cabos Humane Society as shoppers in my store. The timing of the opening of Cabo Dog coincided with the holiday season. And the largest fundraising event of the year for the Humane Society was "Dressed to the K9's". I had heard about it on our previous trips to Cabo. Keith's company had a *posada*—a company Christmas party—each year, so we were always in town the first week of December. But we had never attended any of these affairs, as time was short and his company party was always the main event. But I had read about it and had seen advertisements, so I knew it was coming up.

Several customers had come in looking for particular items for this event, whether it was something to dress their pet in or something to use as part of a pet-themed donation basket. I was hearing a lot about Dressed to the K9's. It was happening on the same night as Keith's company party, but we decided to buy tickets and go afterwards to show our support.

We arrived late, and the party was full and buzzing. It was a welcome surprise that some of the customers recognized me from the store and said hello. We also ran into some of Keith's longtime friends who had been a part of the Cabo scene for many years. The event seemed to be a big success, and I knew we wouldn't want to miss it the next year.

The store stayed open a total of six months. It came as a shock to everyone that so many cruise ships were suddenly dropping Cabo from their ports. There had been some bad press about violence in Mazatlán. The cruise-ship industry is quick to shift gears, and with this recent news, they were no longer offering the same number of cruises for the coming season. The first season my store was open was the best it was going to be. From there, the struggles were written clearly on the wall. With less than half the number of tourists coming to Cabo via cruise ship the coming season, there were some tough decisions to make.

During those months, I had the opportunity to receive positive feedback from my customers. Many offered the suggestion of creating an online store, one that would purvey the image and feel of Cabo Dog but also allow people to purchase items from the United States. With many vendors offering drop shipping as an option, I began to do my research. So as hard as it was to close the brick-and-mortar store, it allowed me to expand and create something where I could reach many more customers. It was a bittersweet ending, but I knew that it had been the best thing for me to do at that time. It was also the only choice in this fast-changing climate of Mexico.

The Longest Summer

AS TIME WENT ON, I fell into a new routine. The store's closure had been hard, but I was fully focused on the new concept of an online store. On weekdays, Keith and I would have breakfast and then he would leave for the office. I would take Roy on his morning walk and then skip off to the office as well. There was plenty to learn about with this online business. Social media, blogging, and preparing newsletters, as well as adding new inventory to the site, were a lot to handle. Outside of work, I kept busy with the usual domestics of shopping, caring for our home, and of course, caring for Roy. I was content.

Summer had rolled around, and as it is in the Baja, things were heating up. The snowbirds had flown off to their summer resting spots. They had other homes in other places where the summer seasons were more manageable. The high season in Cabo and all of its charitable and social events were a thing of the past. Those of us who stayed down south for the summer began to find ways to hunker down and stay cool.

It was midweek, and I needed to run some errands. The road to Costco is the most heavily trafficked road in Cabo. It is the four-lane that runs from the airport to San José del Cabo, and then all the way to Land's End, Cabo San Lucas—and practically everywhere one needs to travel. Going to Costco was just one of the stops. There was also Walmart, Home Depot, and the Santa Carmela Market, which was dubbed the "Trader Joe's of Cabo".

As I was driving out to do my errands that day in July, I noticed them. Across the street from Costco, in a huge open space, were a group of horses. I had not seen them before. I have a keen eye for animals of any type, so I knew they had not been there long. But there they were. And as I drove closer, I could see them gathered along a wood-and-barbwire fence that lined the busy road. As I sat in my car at the red light, waiting to turn, I looked very closely at them. They were standing very still in the hot desert sun, tails flicking left and right. Their necks were stretched out, with the weight of their heads at the end like bobbers. Their eyes were half closed, and they were thin. I counted about six of them at the time. A few were tied to the fence, with ropes around their necks, and the others stood close by.

As the light turned green, I began to drive off. I was perplexed as to why they were out there in the middle of the hot desert all by themselves. The fenced-in area of land must have been twenty acres or so, with no homes or ranches on the property. I'd heard that this land was held by a Mexican family in trust. They were waiting for the right buyer to come along and develop it. But for now, it was a barren desert with nothing else living there but cactus and no water in sight. What business did these horses have out there along the road—in the heat, tied to the fence, on land that was not fit for them? I felt angst with these questions, but I had grown accustomed to seeing animals in questionable conditions before. But this situation was disturbing.

On my shopping errands over the coming weeks, I started seeing this band of horses on each occasion I drove that road. It was god-awful hot, and the longest days of summer were upon us. The horses seemed to be falling weaker and deteriorating quickly in these cruel conditions. I worried for them. Horses in these parts did not live in standards like those back home, but they were not doing well at all. I felt helpless to the situation. I didn't know anyone to contact. And since they were in plain sight of just about everyone in town, I surely wasn't alone in my concern.

One day, I drove by and noticed water buckets and

loose hay that looked as though it had been tossed over the fence. I was relieved to see this, and it lifted my concerns greatly. Up until then, I hadn't really known what the horses were being provided, if anything at all. By the looks of them, any effort being made was meager, to say the least. Their bodies and faces spoke the truth. But seeing the water buckets and hay did give me a thread of hope that whoever they belonged to was trying.

And then, a week later, my concerns deepened again. At the intersection along the busy road where the horses were being held stood a sign. Someone had taken a large sheet of plywood and, with bright-orange spray paint, written the words "horses need food, horses need water." The quick reality set in and registered an alarm that the food and water I had seen were not from the owner of the horses but from good Samaritans. My mind raced, and I thought back to the first time I had seen them, which had been six weeks ago or longer. Had they been suffering this entire time? Had they spent these past weeks in utter starvation, out in the horrendous conditions of the longest summer, with nothing?

I took stock of the situation, and the full weight of it hit me hard. My stomach turned over and over again. I drove into Costco, parked, and looked across the busy road at them. I wanted to wrap my arms around them and take them home, or take them to safety. But I'd learned just enough about living in the Baja by now to know that there was no one to call, no one to help—I had learned this one the hard way with Señor Giraffe. But nonetheless, that is exactly what I wanted to do. I wanted to save them. My eyes filled with tears. They were just melting away in the desert sun. They were held captive in a hell of heat, humidity, and a lack of humanity. Where was the humanity in all of this?

Señor Giraffe

YEARS EARLIER, on one of my first visits to Cabo, I came across Señor Giraffe. This was not his real name, of course. I never did learn his real name, or if he even had one. But Señor Giraffe was the name I had given him, which is something I do when I see animals around but never have the chance to be formally introduced—and this was the case with Señor Giraffe.

Keith's office building was in a commercial district of Cabo. It was very close to the main road and the ocean. But it was in a commercially zoned area. The roads were mostly dirt, and the properties were sectioned off into *hectares*. Each property was approximately 107,000 square feet, or 2.2 acres.

A lot of these commercial spaces had yet to be built on. The people who owned them used them for any number of things. Keith had built a large two-story *bodega*, which was where his company was located. On one side of Keith's bodega was a building owned by an American who had a company that installed hurricane shutters. And across the street was a small brickmaking factory. There was a hospital at the turn from the main road to the office. So there were lots of different things built, with open space in between them. Some of these plots of land had yet to be turned into any real business, but they had loads of stuff on them. Some resembled junkyards with old vehicles, containers, or even boats.

Keith and I were driving back to the office one afternoon, and as we turned from the main road to go to the bodega, we saw a horse running down the dirt road. He was a palomino-colored horse and looked to be a few years old. He had long limbs and a long gangly neck, which is why I called him Señor Giraffe. He seemed to be in good spirits, trotting around, yet I did notice a rope around his neck. But as I had seen earlier, the folks in the area loved to tie up their horses, even in fields with fences.

Across the big road was an established horse-riding place, and it seemed logical that he had somehow gotten onto the wrong side of the street and was enjoying this little exploration. I didn't give it much thought, assuming his owners would soon come and take him back across the street to join all the others. This place seemed to take fair care of their horses, so it didn't cause me any concern. It was just a horse running down the road—another day in Cabo.

A few months passed, and I was back down in Cabo with Keith on a business trip. I was in the car, leaving the bodega to run some errands, and decided to drive a different direction than what I normally would. I was into exploring a bit, and this seemed like a nice detour.

As I turned down the street and did my best to avoid the large ruts in the dirt road, I noticed a familiar figure up ahead of me. As I got closer, I could see what looked like a horse, swinging his tail to and fro. But it was so odd because I didn't see much else. Then the dust cleared, I got close enough to see the horrible sight, and my heart sank.

It was Señor Giraffe. But the beautiful horse I had seen was now pure skin and bones, tied to a boat in a yard. He had no food or water, just tied there like a post that had been set in the ground. From his back side, besides his swaying tail, he didn't look like a horse at all. His body was so concave that his butt didn't come anywhere near rubbing together. There was no belly that stuck out on either side. He was rail thin, a wisp of the horse I had seen a few months earlier. How in God's name did someone just tie him up and leave him to die like this?

His head was down, and he looked at peace. He was not crying for help or even looking distressed. He was nibbling on some thin green blades of grass that had grown up around the boat he called home. And, ever so slowly, his tail swayed back and forth in the breeze of the tropical air. I felt as though I could hear his heart beat with every breath he took. I could see his ribs expand and contract. This horse that was a mere shadow of the beautiful, young, strong horse I'd seen a few months earlier was now hanging on to life by a thread.

He was on a property inside a hectare, and it was completely fenced off. With all my might, I wanted to take hold of his rope and lead him away from that boat, lead him somewhere, anywhere. But that was not the law of this land. This horse was a possession of the owner of the property. He could do whatever he chose to this animal, and there was not one law that said otherwise. The cold hard truth of a world I did not know set in, and I felt utterly helpless. Señor Giraffe had no one. A voiceless soul was soon to become another casualty of this rough and wild land.

I went back to the office and told Keith what I had seen. His face hardened into an expression of anger. He was not as shocked as I was but still angered by this situation. I told him we needed to call the Humane Society, someone, to come help this horse. I knew the Humane Society existed for small-animal rescue. But were horses part of the equation? I called and the man who answered the phone listened to my plea for help. He then told me that the Humane Society didn't handle large-animal cases and that he was very sorry. He asked where the horse was, and I did my best to describe it to him. And that was it. He said again that he was sorry.

So I left it at that. For the remainder of the trip, I was haunted by Señor Giraffe's presence. I prayed for him to be rescued, and I could only take comfort in the small blades of grass he had in front of him. Maybe they tried to feed him but he was sick? I gave myself whatever antidote I needed to accept that this was happening and there was nothing I could do about it.

We flew home and, a few days later, learned that Tom—the neighbor with the hurricane-shutter business—had asked the man who owned the horse to give him water. He did, but it didn't take but a few weeks before Señor Giraffe was gone.

I later learned that the man I spoke to at the Humane Society had found Señor Giraffe and tried to speak to the owner. As a fellow Cabo local, he tried his best to convince the man to let him take the horse. He, too, was a horse lover. And even though the Humane Society doesn't handle large-animal cases, he went out there on a personal mission to help this animal—but to no avail. The owner wasn't going to let someone else take his possession. There was no changing his mind. It was hard for me to accept my lack of power in the face of cruelty here in this land. And I can only imagine how much it pained the kind man who had tried his best. Even in his own country, he'd had to grow a thick skin—but mine was still tender.

The Longest Summer Continues

I TOOK MY SHOPPING LIST and tromped into Costco. Filled with hate and anger, I was simply beside myself. I felt hopelessly lost once again as the old scars and pain of Señor Giraffe grabbed my heart. It was another slap in the face by reality, and it left me red. As Señor Giraffe passed through my mind, I couldn't fathom the thought that these horses might meet the same ending. Something had to be done. Someone had to save them from this fate.

I returned to the office and shared what I had learned with Keith. His face sank and his heart was heavy. I could see that he wasn't that surprised, although he felt terrible for them. But I could see pity for me as well. He knew that I was still so fresh in this place, still working to learn this hard lesson. He did his best to protect me from this truth. But the harsh reality of the world around us could not be swept away. It was raw. It was real, and it was utterly breaking my heart.

When I went home that night, Roy and I walked in the shade of the setting sun. Pedregal is situated on a mountain that looks out towards the Pacific Ocean and the Sea of Cortez, the blending of two beautiful oceans at one sharp and buffered mass of land. These two different seas have a way of roaring into each other, one cold with water from the north and the other warm with salty water from the south. They blend together as nature intended. I felt defeated, learning of the plight of the horses. My internal conflict was like that of the two oceans crashing into one another. I wanted to understand this culture and to blend in, but I had such a strong emotional disconnect from this place that it was painful. My mind was searching for ways to accept the situation, but my heart was crying out. I knew I had to be strong and find a way to blend into this new world. If I didn't, I would be swept away, back to where I started when I arrived here. The lessons I had learned would bear no meaning. So I decided to throw my shoulders back and not crumble. I would stand strong against the tides.

From that moment forward, I prayed every night before bed. I clasped my hands hard and grimaced as I spoke the words, asking to find safety for the horses. I prayed for someone to help them. And I prayed for someone to help me understand this culture and hold back the anger that was beginning to burrow inside me. I was home, safe with Keith and Roy, inside our home on the hill, behind the private gates and walls that created a comfortable world. I took into account who I was and all that I had to be thankful for. And I prayed just once more. Because it was becoming all too clear to me that beyond this bubble was a harsh new world that was revealing itself to me in bits and pieces. And beyond those walls, I was helpless to it. And those horses? They were helpless too.

I began to take any occasion to drive out on the four-lane and check in on them. Some days, they would be right where I expected them to be, lined up—some tied, some loose—near the fence where the sign was and where the good Samaritans had been leaving them food and water. I started to notice one particular horse who stood out amongst the others: a fiery little red gelding with a large white fishhook blaze down the front of his face. He was thin like the rest, but he had a different look in his eyes. He must have been weak, in such pain. Yet he held his head high with his eyes wide open, on full alert. I once saw him trotting through the lot adjacent to where they were being held, running towards an acacia tree to eat. He must have escaped, and I saw hope in his eyes. He was later returned to the herd. But he had a fire in his soul that told me he was a fighter. While the others appeared to be in a state of surrender, this horse was not going down without a fight. He became the face I prayed for each night. As much as the entire group needed help, this little red fireball with the fishhook blaze was the one I thought of and the one I began to look for in particular. He carried the last bit of hope and strength for the herd. And I recognized his courage. He gave me hope.

Gringo Gazette

IN CABO, WE HAD NO NEWS NETWORK on television. The radio was in Spanish, and the news generated there was hard for me to decipher. There was no reliable source of news in English. But there was a paper called the *Gringo Gazette*.

As you might imagine by the name, the *Gringo Gazette* is a collection of news and stories generated to serve—yes, you guessed it—the expat community. In my opinion, the stories can at times have a bit of spin or read as somewhat abrupt. People learn to understand the humor with stories by authors such as Sandy Beach or Penny Wise. It is a colorful paper with a dedicated owner and staff who take a story and write it with a sprinkle of sass.

The paper is published every two weeks like clockwork and is a welcome resource the ex-pat community enjoys. It is distributed around town in many restaurants and cafes where most of the gringos frequent. *Gringo* is a word used to describe those of us from the north. A typical gringo can be found wearing flip-flops, shorts, a T-shirt or beach cover-up, a floppy hat, and sunglasses. They will most likely be pink-skinned from too much time in the sun and red-eyed from too much tequila. And they will be smiling, as mostly all gringos in Cabo are happy, delightful types who are living their dreams. Away from all the hustle and bustle of the developed nations, they can now be found meandering through life without so much as a care in the world.

I stopped in for a coffee one morning on my way to the office. Cabo Coffee was a landmark place with a reputation for strong coffee, the kind that will take an edge off a hangover—which is why many gringos frequent it.

I greeted the staff with a cheerful "buenos días" and ordered my coffee in Spanish. The line wasn't moving fast, as there were always a few tourists who were floundering around with their words and their pesos. So while I waited for my coffee, I grabbed a copy of the GG.

I scanned the front page, and my mouth dropped when I saw the cover story. On the front of that week's copy was a large photo of a group of horses. Most of the horses in the photo hung their heads low. But one horse in particular captured my attention: one red, angry-faced horse holding his head high in protest of his current situation. While the others looked as though they waved a white flag in surrender, this horse stood strongly planted and upright with a fight in his eyes. As I looked past his face, I saw the thin, bony body. He was outstretched over a barbwire fence as though he was leading the charge. And apparently he was, for himself and for the others. He looked mad as hell, and he was ready to tell the world about it. I looked closer at the picture, and then I saw the wooden sign, the same one I had seen at Costco, with large, orange spray-painted letters: "horses need food, horses need water." This horse stood next to the sign as if he understood the words. It was his call to action. He looked as though he was saying "It's about time, people."

I took the paper, collected my latte, and sat down to read the article. The story was indeed about the Costco horses—the same horses I had seen on numerous occasions, the horses I first thought were well before learning that they were dying in front of all of us on the busiest road in Cabo, and the same horses we could do nothing about. The laws in this land protected their owner and did nothing to protect the precious creatures who had no voice. They allowed people to treat living beings as a commodity. As soon as something was of no use to them, they could park it and walk away—the tires deflating, the chains rusting, just park it and walk away. And that was exactly the case here. These horses had been parked and forgotten.

The article was straightforward. It told how the laws worked and how unfortunate it was for the horses, as the man who owned them had too big an ego to ask for or accept help. It was his right to park them there in the heat of the desert without so much as a flake of hay or bucket of water. He could make the choice to do this, and there was absolutely nothing anyone could do, except for publicly shaming him into doing better. And that was exactly what the paper intended to do. It was the only way any of us could get them the help they needed. Perhaps public shaming would create an opening for someone to come in and help these animals. It was the only tool we had.

As I read the article, I realized that time was of the essence. The horses were now on the radar of the saints of Cabo who spent precious time and money doing what they could to bring hope and a future to those who needed it. I felt it was a lucky card for them, and now that the entire community was aware of this, something big would happen. It had to. I felt hope for them. But by no means were they out of the woods. For now, the food and water that was being supplied for them over the fence would have to do. We would have to wait for something bigger to happen.

The Horses' Disappearance

WITHIN WEEKS OF THE ARTICLE being published, the horses disappeared. We had spent some time visiting family in California, and when we returned home, the horses were gone. I felt relieved that this had finally ended for them. I was sure the paper had roused the attention of someone with some tact who had gotten the owner to relinquish the animals to them. I pictured the horses being taken to a safe haven. I imagined green pastures and a safe place where they would be provided with love, nurturing, and an abundance of fresh food and water. I pictured kind faces of people now caring for them. I felt the relief they must have felt with finally being rescued.

My drive along the highway now was no longer filled with angst and anxiety. I no longer saw the horses struggling along the road, waiting for their lives to be saved. It had come to an end, and my heart now took long sighs of relief as I passed the Costco corner. The summer had been long and hot, and as the days grew shorter, I began to forget about them. Life went on, and somewhere out there, they were mending their broken bodies. And I was mending my broken heart as I grew faith in our community, knowing that somehow they had pulled off a miracle—or so we thought.

Dressed to the K9's

IT WAS DECEMBER NOW, and the high season was just
beginning to unfold. The annual Dressed to the K9's was
always held the first weekend of December. The party was
on a Saturday night. I had gone shopping at the fancy
Puerto Paraiso Mall and found a ruby-red dress with silver and black sequins, simple yet chic. In the afternoon,
I had gone to the salon and had my hair done, and as I
drove home, the sun was just beginning to set. The air
was warm and dry, a much-needed change after such a
long and relentlessly hot summer. Everything felt calm,
quiet, and still. Keith was dressed in his khaki shorts and
a white linen long-sleeved button-down shirt. He was
freshly shaven and looked as though he'd walked out of a
Tommy Bahama catalog.

After I dressed, we shared a glass of champagne on
the patio, chatting lightly about this and that. Roy lazed
at our feet and was respectful of our Dressed to the K9's
apparel. I felt a sense of calmness and quiet that I had
been missing. Summer had been long, hot, and uncomfortable, to say the least. But as the seasons changed and
the days grew shorter and cooler, my attitude improved.
Summers had always felt this way to me. I am one of
those people who relish the time when we say goodbye to
the hot weather. And living here, so far south, I just felt a
completely new spirit arise.

The party was less than a five-minute drive from our
house. It was within walking distance, but not in high
heels. We valeted the car and sauntered along the cobble-
stone street to the entrance. For several years now, the
location for the event was at a grand estate situated on

the beach of the Pedregal. It had a look and feel of regality, with sweeping floor-to-ceiling windows that led to the breathtaking Pacific Ocean, surrounded by the drastic rock cliffs the Pedregal is famous for. It was a beautiful setting.

Keith and I wandered through the crowd. It was nice to see some familiar faces. My time at Cabo Dog had introduced me to some of these folks, as well as others we had come to know personally and built friendships with. The combination of new friends mixed with old, whom Keith had known for many years, left me feeling warmhearted.

Keith began to talk with a man he knew but hadn't seen in some time. Like Keith, this friend had moved from the States many years ago and started a new life in Cabo. After some brief chitchat, he introduced us to his date, Elizabeth. She was a tall woman with long, thick hair. Elizabeth shook my hand with a vigor that gave me a glimpse into the strength of her personality. We talked as the guys enjoyed their time reconnecting.

She and I covered the usual topics. How long have you lived in Cabo? How did you know about this event? After this brief exchange, it didn't take long to see that she had something she wanted to get off her chest.

Elizabeth was not the kind of person to hide emotion. The topic of animals in need soon led to her story of a recent rescue of her own. I listened and waited on every word as she told me her story.

She had been away for a few months to visit family in Canada during the late summer. She returned to Cabo and began riding again. She kept a horse named Carlos at a barn not too far from town. Someone had told her about some horses in desperate need of help. She and her friend went to investigate and soon found them, a small herd of horses in very poor condition.

Elizabeth had been in Cabo for many years, and she knew immediately who these horses belonged too. The owner had a reputation for neglect, so that was a day when she could not turn a blind eye. She and her friend went back to her barn, collected her horse trailer, and set out to rescue someone. After negotiations and paperwork, notaries, and signatures, she collected the worst of them. One small red gelding was held in a pen no larger than a chicken coop. His head hung low to the ground, and he was so weak that she had to pick up each hoof to get him into the trailer. She loaded him up and drove him the two miles to her barn, which happened to have just one stall available. Without so much as notifying the barn manager, she took this starving sack of bones to her safe haven. From there, he would begin his journey back to health.

I sat and listened to her story in complete silence. She was so matter-of-fact about the whole thing—it was almost as if it had been all in a day's work. But I knew that underneath her strength and matter-of-factness was her vulnerability. I could tell that she had a heart of gold and that under that strong exterior was a soft and special woman. I asked her how I could help, and her reply was "Well, you could feed him!" It was as if she was in denial herself about her heroic actions. But one thing was certain: She was not the kind of lady who would take bullshit from anyone, including a local who didn't treat his horses right. It was a win for the little red gelding.

I didn't have any magical words of wisdom or anything to offer except to give her my phone number. I told her to contact me if I could help in any way. She was obviously still reconciling the fact that she now had two horses, two mouths to feed. She had many connections and depth in this community, so she was confident she would find what she needed to help her rescue horse. But by offering my number, at least she would know I valued what she had done for that animal. And if she needed me, she could reach out anytime.

As the food was being served, Elizabeth and her date went their own way. Keith and I had high expectations for a night of friends and wine and dancing, so we went our own way to continue with the festivities. It was hard to focus as I wondered about all these other heroes in the group. How many others there had faced such challenges to save creatures' lives? I certainly had a few dog rescues under my belt. But how was it that I met the one woman who had rescued a horse? I am always one who believes in fate. Something about this woman and her red rescue horse resonated in my heart.

New Year's 2013

THE NEW YEAR HOLIDAY is a really special holiday for me. I love this time to reflect back on a year and see where it has taken us, and also the ability to turn it over and put it to rest. Some years are good and some not so good. The beauty of the New Year is to choose it, own it, and then bid farewell to it and turn the calendar. It is an opportunity to hit the refresh button.

This had been my first full year living abroad. Keith and I had gone through some growing pains. But we had also grown closer in ways I hadn't imagined. He really stepped up for me and was such a strong shoulder to lean on while I fiddled around learning a new way of life. He was a good listener, which wasn't easy, because I had been pretty good at complaining. But after this first full year, I felt more centered and part of this town now. I was ready to celebrate!

Nick-San Sushi is a true gem in Cabo. It's an institution of core Japanese sushi preparation paired with the flavors of the Baja. The combinations are mouthwatering and the service is impeccable. Nick-San was the perfect place to ring in the New Year.

We spent three hours eating, drinking, and laughing that night. We wore the glitter top hat and tiara that were handed out to us, and we blew our horns with joy. The restaurant was full to the brim, and it was prime time for people watching. A large group of professional hockey players with their model girlfriends took over one corner. The beautiful people were on spot that night. When the clock struck twelve, the crowd cheered and roared. We laughed and kissed and swayed with delight. I felt as though the night would never end. And as I pondered the year of the past, I was certain we were heading for something special.

The following day was lazy. We took Roy for a walk to the beach and watched as whales breached on the glistening ocean. The air was warm and clean and fresh. I breathed it in as fuel for my soul.

We went to a late lunch on the marina. People and children strolled by at a slow pace. Whistles blew as the children tried to sell them to passersby. The Christmas tree was still in the corner. Dry and brittle, it looked hungover as well.

We snacked on chips as we waited for our burgers to arrive. A wonderful thing in Cabo, chips and salsa are always on the table. I was taking a bite when I suddenly felt a long, hot pain in my lower jaw. I guessed it had been a hard chip and took a long sip of my margarita.

We ate our lunch, and although I could manage, the pain was quite peculiar. At one moment, it would be in the front lower jaw and then the next, the upper right. It was gone and then back again. It was hot and hard, and then it was tingling and pressing. It was something I had never experienced before. It was just not right.

The pain continued on and off for the rest of that day. I chalked it up to the tortilla chips and assumed it would pass with time. And it did. By the following morning, the pain had simply vanished.

Tomatoes Meeting

ONE AFTERNOON IN FEBRUARY, I had plans with two of my close friends. The Los Cabos Tomatoes is a women's social group. With hundreds of members and meetings every other week, it is well known in Cabo. We had planned to attend meetings at some of the more attractive venues. This day's event was no exception. A new hotel had opened, and the restaurant was welcoming us for a tour, wine, and hors d'oeuvres. What better way to spend a lovely afternoon?

The girls came to our house, and I drove from there. After Roy enjoyed his licks and tail wags, and kisses from them, we piled into my Jeep and set off to the Montecristo.

It was every bit as amazing as we had expected. The party was set at the newly constructed clubhouse that perched out facing the vast Pacific Ocean. In the distance, we could see a grassy knoll with white tents, chairs, and linens. The women had given special attention to dressing up for this occasion. There was music and wine, sunshine and laughter. I felt so lucky that the three of us could enjoy such a nice event.

The afternoon was winding down, and it was time for us to leave. We got in my Jeep and began the slow drive up the winding road. There was a steady stream of conversation, and I was listening to them talk about the party when I felt a sudden excruciating pain on my back. I thought something must have been biting me. My first instinct was to stop the car and jump out quickly, and I began to flail my sundress to-and-fro, trying to rid myself of the stinging pain. The girls looked at me in confusion. I tried to explain what I was feeling as best I could, and I asked them to look closely at my back to tell me what they could see. The stinging, stabbing pain continued. And after they looked very closely, they told me, "Christie, we can't see anything." I hardly believed them, as the pain felt the size of an orange and had to be from a bite of some kind. But again they told me there was not so much as a small red bump to be seen. And then, just as suddenly as the pain had started, it vanished—again. It completely disappeared without leaving a trace of the stinging sensation. I was completely bewildered by this. And as I got back in the car to drive home, the conversation that was once lively and carefree was now shrouded in silence. We were all perplexed by this, and as much as I was concerned about what had just happened, so, too, were my friends.

The months went by, and soon we were at the forefront of summer again. The temperatures were creeping up ever so steadily. Even though I had not experienced any other alarming pains, other things had begun to catch my attention. I noticed a weakness in my left leg. At times, it would fold when taking a step. My balance, once strong and steady, began to waver. My depth perception was challenged. I would reach for the refrigerator door, but it would take three attempts for my hand to grab it. I was feeling all sorts of odd, piercing pains in my face, cheeks, nose, lips, or ears. There was the vibration that would take over my body and then vanish. I had sensations of warm water dripping down my legs, or the feeling that I had just crossed through sprinklers. Some of these were subtle and some not so subtle. As the days grew hotter and longer, so did all the weird sensations.

Telling Keith

THE WEEKENDS IN CABO were mostly spent at the beach. Keith's schedule had him working Monday through Friday and a half day on Saturday. I kept busy with my routine during the week as well. But come about two o'clock on Saturday, it was time to head to the shore.

Medano Beach is the main beach in Cabo. It sits on a beautiful bay that is sculpted by the magnificent Land's End and the famous Arch on one side and then wraps around in a perfect crescent to the other side. The entrance to the marina is situated at the mouth of the bay, and the strip of beach that fronts the opposite side runs endlessly south. This bay was once the home of a fishing cannery in the 1920s. In the 1970s, Cabo became known for its proximity to world-class fishing. And for many years, that was what carried it through periods of growth and development. But as flights increased and the word got out that this place had more to offer than just fishing, Cabo began to boom.

Medano Beach has some of the oldest and nicest hotels in Cabo. The natural bay offers gentle tides of crystal-blue and green water perfect for swimming. The hotels there are also within walking distance to town and have some of the best restaurants in the Baja. Over time, the development and sprawl of the Baja has moved north and south. But to those who know Medano Beach and the grand bay with El Arco, it is the original quintessential essence of Cabo, and loved and cherished by many.

At the far end of the beach sits a two-story hotel named Cascadas. In Spanish, this means "waterfalls." The first of the Cascadas hotels was built in Puerta Vallarta, along a rugged cliff. The architect designed the villas to have pools that, when seen from a distance, appeared like pools of a waterfall. The name continued to the development in Cabo. It is one of the smallest hotels on Medano Beach. But what Cascadas lacks in stature, it makes up for in heart.

This was where we spent almost all our beach time. In front of the hotel sat a large *palapa* restaurant. And between the palapa and the shore were a handful of tables and umbrellas. Keith's back injury made it difficult for him to sit on a lounge chair for very long, so we found that the beachside table and chairs in the sand made the perfect setting for afternoons at the beach.

The service at Cascadas was incredible. The food was unforgettable, and the view was priceless. We ordered our usual bucket of beer to quench our thirst and then an order of the ceviche, which was served in a blown-glass martini glass that was clear with a traditional Mexican blue rim, chock-full of fresh shrimp, octopus, scallops, and fish mixed with a mouthwatering tangy tomato sauce and then topped off with fresh lime and avocado, house-made chips, and pico de gallo. Our favorite server, Rafael, had arrived for his afternoon shift just in time to make us his house-made guacamole tableside.

It was early May, and we were enjoying an amazing day. Keith and I are talkers of every subject, and this day was no different. As we chatted about this and that, I mentioned some of the odd sensations and pains I had been noticing: the weakness in my leg and the sharp pains that had no explanation. He listened very intently and asked me some questions. Did I have an allergy to something? Maybe I'd caught a bug that could be wreaking havoc on my body? Neither of us could come up with anything that made sense. It was the first time I had told anyone about how terribly I had been feeling. Quite honestly, I felt silly listening to myself try to describe it all. By telling him and confiding in him, it became real that there could be something really wrong with me. He expressed his concern. I almost wished I could take back all the words and return to keeping it my secret. But I knew that would not serve anyone, and by telling Keith, we could now figure this out together. We decided I would call my primary care doctor back in the States first thing Monday morning. Yes, it was time to investigate this further.

Appointment with Dr. Roland

I FLEW UP TO PARK CITY the first of June. After I had explained the things I was feeling to the nurse over the phone, she instructed me to come for a visit. She told me to plan to be there long enough for any necessary testing. It was summer, and Keith was swamped at work. It was no time for me to be needy, so I bucked up and planned a trip for the week. I would go by myself.

Going to a doctor appointment with some unknown symptoms was nerve-racking, but having to leave home and travel by myself back to the States made me feel more glum about things.

I arrived late on a Monday night after a painfully long three-hour delay in Denver. With the lack of sleep and stress from the travel day before, I woke up jittery and nervous on Tuesday. My appointment with Dr. Roland was at ten o'clock in the morning. *Good*, I could get a cup of coffee and shake off my nerves.

I arrived on time and was quickly taken into the exam room. The nurse took my temperature and gathered my weight and my blood pressure. She asked why I was there to see Dr. Roland, and I told her, "I have a lot of different kinds of things going on that I want to talk to her about." Where else was I to start? The odd sensations and weaknesses ran the gamut. I decided to save the list for Dr. Roland herself.

I'd always liked Dr. Roland. She was a straight shooter who didn't hesitate to cover all the bases. I felt confident that she would be very thorough and would leave no stone unturned.

She asked me some basic formalities, and then we jumped right in. I ran down the list I had been keeping on my iPhone, telling her all the oddball things I had been noticing. She listened carefully, watching me intently. She asked me if I'd fallen. And she had questions about my balance. And then she said, "Well, you know, when you have such a diffuse range of symptoms like this, the first thing I am concerned about is MS." MS. Multiple Sclerosis. I myself had come across this quite a few times in my mad Googling of symptoms. But to hear her say it sounded an alarm, big time. She explained that with the body, when there is pain in one general region, they can look at reasons relating to that physical area. But the fact that I had pains and sensations ranging from the top of my head to the tips of my toes made her want to address MS right away.

She didn't hesitate in ordering a full MRI scan of my brain and neck regions. They would contact my insurance company to get authorization and work on getting me on the schedule that week, as I told her I was going home on Saturday. She smiled, closed my file, and then walked me to reception.

The hospital called to schedule me after they received the necessary authorization. The MRI was set for the following morning. As the nurse went over the procedures with me, she also asked some questions. I told her this was my first MRI, so she went on to give me the details. The procedure could take up to three hours, as they would be doing a full workup. MRIs are performed using a large magnetic resonance imaging system. It is imperative to hold perfectly still during the procedure so as not to skew the images.

First I would lie comfortably on a table that then slid into the belly of the machine, but not before the technicians propped my head and neck to prevent me from moving. They would then give me an IV so that at the end of the procedure, they could inject a contrast for the last round of images. The whole process sounded extremely restricting. And for someone who was claustrophobic, it was going to be terrifying. I envisioned three hours of hell. I called Dr. Roland and asked if she would order some sort of sedative for me.

The test went fine. I was falling asleep in the waiting room as soon as I had dressed in the gown they gave me—a perfectly sedated patient ready and willing to do my duty as instructed. Yes, the valium had done its job.

Less than three hours later, I was finished. I checked out with the nurse and walked to the coffee shop. The sun was moving west, and the sky was turning a pale color of yellow. I was a long way from home in Cabo, but yet I was comforted by my surroundings. The mountains had always made me feel safe and secure. Now all I could do was sit tight and wait it out.

Back in Cabo

I FLEW HOME THAT SATURDAY. Keith picked me up from the airport, and it was so good to see him. As we drove the forty-five minutes back home, I told him about my visit. We caught up on what had happened in Cabo that week. I described the day of the test and how it had gone, but we didn't talk about the possibility of MS. Keith firmly believed in dealing with facts, so until we had something to base things on, there was no real reason to hypothesize. But I felt different than when I left, like I had picked up a new weight to carry, a weight that no one around me could feel. So I kept my wondering to myself.

Roy greeted me with a great big, crooked smile and waggy tail. He always made the cutest grunting sounds after I'd been away from home. He seemed to be as content as Keith with picking up life exactly where it left off. I decided this was a good course of action, for now at least.

After a quick walk with Roy and Keith, we drove down to Cascadas to catch the late-afternoon activity. Our routine and the familiar surroundings brought me such comfort. The weight lifted ever so slightly.

Living in Cabo had its share of challenges. Technology was always a day late and a dollar short of what we were accustomed to in the US. This made communication challenging, to say the least—especially when waiting on pins and needles to hear from the doctor about an important test result.

Our cell phones were international numbers, so I had given the office our Vonage numbers, which were US phone numbers. About a week later, Dr. Roland tried to contact me by calling our office number. I got the message as it was transcribed through the system, and those were never very clear. After reading her name and the phone number on the email message, I knew exactly what it was about, so I drove home to call her back from our house phone. It was getting late in the day, and I hoped she hadn't gone home for the day.

When I called, the nurse told me she would have to call me back. *OK then, I would be patient. Nothing to worry about*, I told myself. I turned on the news and fiddled around the house. Roy was watching me with a careful eye, as it was getting dangerously close to his walking time, which was even closer to his dinnertime. And, well, dinnertime was the highlight of this Labrador's day. So as much as I was trying to be patient, his panting and incessant shadow put me even more on edge.

The phone rang and I answered. Dr. Roland explained to me that the test results from the MRI had come back and showed something evidentiary of MS. She was going to need to refer me to a specialist. Dr. Peters was a neurologist at the University of Utah MS Clinic and had an outstanding reputation, so she was going to refer me to him for follow-up.

After we hung up, I sat on the sofa with the air conditioner blowing and a large Labrador panting in my ear. Yet I heard nothing but silence. I felt like I was being swallowed up. The weight I had been carrying around so cautiously the past several days suddenly went cascading down off my shoulders and landed squarely in my lap—a crash landing that had me all in bits. I hung my head down between my knees and started to cry. It was a quiet cry, or at least I didn't hear myself sobbing. Roy leaned in very gently and licked my cheek with the tippy tip of his large slobbery tongue. He, too, seemed rocked by this news, and he approached me with great care and concern. That was not what I had wanted to hear. Not at all.

Like anyone, I'd had times in my life when I feared the worst, but slid through by the skin of my chin to a positive outcome. And there had been times when I expected the best and willed myself to no other outcome but a good one. But then, when something took a turn down an unwanted path, I crumbled. That's where I was now standing—at the beginning of a journey I did not want to take. And there was no detour in sight. I had no choice but to go forward, down that lost and lonely road.

And any useful tools that I had for strength in the past were nowhere in sight. They were all back home in the US—our friends and family who would no doubt be of great help during this time, the anchors who steady us during the tough times. All my anchors were a thousand miles up the Baja. They were across an international border, living separate lives from the one we were experiencing. That is, all my anchors except for two: Keith, and Roy were there, and I would have to lean on them now more than ever. But would they be enough? And was it fair to ask this of them? I had been through some tough times in my life when I felt alone. But this time, the sense of isolation and disconnect was beyond anything I had experienced before. I did not want to be a burden. I did not want to take this detour in life to a great unknown.

Waiting

THE CLINIC FOR NEUROSCIENCES contacted me, and after a very lengthy review, I was finally approved to see Dr. Peters. The first available appointment was December 16. That was six months away! In some ways, I felt relieved that they didn't view my situation as urgent. But on the other hand, I wanted some answers. "Idle time is the work of the devil", they say. That combined with Google at my fingertips was clearly a recipe for disaster. I had to stay calm and keep my wits about me. It was going to be another long summer.

That simple approach to facing a devastating diagnosis started to seem trivial to me. While there was no reason to waste a good worry, waking up each day and pushing the what-ifs out of my mind was daunting. Keith did well to keep me on track, going about our lives in general fashion. He's an enthusiastic guy who loves to talk. And with all the new projects going on in Cabo, it was a nice diversion for me. Roy and I were closer than ever, and I also relied heavily on him for distractions. Our morning walks to the beach offered me a tranquil time to reflect and be appreciative of the little things. He was nine years old now, and had enough energy to make it up and down the hill to the beach without too much effort, yet he was old enough to seem to understand the necessity of stopping to smell the flowers. The comfort of our routine and the beauty around me was a blessing. I continued to dive into the online business and did my best to keep my mind from wandering too far in the wrong direction. But the worry and concern were always with me.

In August, three of my closest friends since high school came to Cabo to visit. I was so excited to see them and spend time together. I had told them about what was going on with the doctors and recent tests. Although we had talked on the phone, I was in desperate need of some girl time. I had become aware of my lack of energy, though, and wondered if I would be able to keep up with these girls. The heat of August was taking so much out of me.

As I learned later, MS can cause extreme fatigue. It can be debilitating for some people. The messages in the brain get skewed, and it takes more energy to tell the body what to do. And the heat creates further complications since the insulation around the nerves has been damaged by MS, which further exacerbates the problem. But I vowed to push through and knew they would understand.

Roy smiling amongst the Bouganvilla in Cabo

We had a great time. Three days with three of my closest friends really lifted my spirits. I hated to see them leave, and although I knew I belonged with Keith and Roy, I longed to go back to the States with them. If I could board the plane and go back to California, then maybe I could go back in time, to a place that didn't involve a scary future. I envied them for their simple lives with work schedules and kids' soccer tournaments. Their visit had lifted me, but as soon as they left, I started to flatline again.

The days go by slowly in Cabo. It is part of the charm, I guess. People move at a slower pace. Any of the ordinary things take a bit more time. The fast-paced life in the States was to be laid to rest. Here, people could move at a snail's pace and no one would take notice. But when they want to speed things up by finding things to fill their day, it's not so easy. I did my best not to Google or join chats about MS. But each time I felt a new twinge, or sharp pain, or weakness, my concern grew. I was reminded that this journey I was on could have some real bumps in the road. Between periods of neurotic worry and completely hardened denial, the time did pass.

Telling Dad

IN SEPTEMBER, I went to visit my family in San Diego for a few days. My mom had now been living there since moving back the previous year. Her dementia had caught up with her, and it had become necessary for her to live in a home where she would be safe and cared for. My mom was only seventy-two. She was the youngest-looking resident in her home and seemed to be aware of that. Gentle and kind by nature, she was a welcome resident at Oakdale.

My dad and his wife lived in Tucson and were going to stay at a beach house in San Diego for a week. My brother Mike and his wife, Victoria, were from northern California and would be joining them at the beach house. And my brother Tony and his wife, Cindy, lived in San Diego and would be there as well. The last time I had seen Dad was when he came to Keith's and my wedding reception years earlier. I knew I needed to take the opportunity to go visit.

I spoke to my brother Tony often. He and Cindy were aware of my upcoming doctor appointment and the possibility of MS. My other brother, Mike, however, did not know about this. The day before we were to meet at Dad's, we all got together for lunch. Mom's friend Cathy picked her up, so she was there as well. At lunch, I told Mike about my recent health issues. He was generally concerned, and I appreciated that. I put on a brave face, and with my usual approach of laughing in times of worry, I laid the whole thing to rest so that we could continue to catch up without making it all about me.

The following night, we all gathered at the beach house for one of my dad's famous dinners. He loved to cook and could have been an amazing chef. From an early age, I saw his passion for food as he pulled an octopus out of the ocean in the south of Spain and cooked it on the grill, or ordered shrimp with their heads still on at roadside restaurants in France. Escargot, sushi, unidentified beef skewers, Greek chicken, and a steak that Fred Flintstone would envy—my dad knew how to eat. He lived an adventurous life, and his approach to food was but one example of the larger-than-life man he was. We had an incredible dinner of Dad's homemade lasagna, garlic bread, and bottles of Chianti. I had brought a birthday cake to celebrate Mike's birthday. Once the candles were blown out and the songs had been sung, we retired to the patio and watched the bonfire.

My two brothers, our dad, and I were alone at one point, and Dad looked at me and said, "Chris, is there something you wanted to tell me?" He'd always called me Chris since I was a little girl, and I always felt special that he had a name for me that no one else used—except my mom at times, but it never sounded the same. His voice was high but soft and hesitant. And I immediately sensed a level of concern. I looked at Mike, who just shrugged his shoulders and raised his hands with a guilty expression.

My poor dad looked so worried. Yes, I was his little girl. And he had always protected me. He had kept me safe all these years. I had a rough start as a child. And compared to most children, I caused my parents a lot of worry. I was born with a clubfoot and needed corrective surgery to straighten out my leg. My dad loved those stories of me running through the house with my brothers and then making a quick pivot on the ball of my foot with my half cast. When he told the story, his eyes flickered with happiness. He knew that I was a fighter inside.

There was the time Dad's pet crow took a bite out of my small toe when Mom had me sunbathing on the lawn. That caused an infection that went up into my groin, and I needed surgery to remove the cyst from my lymph gland. I spent five days in the hospital, inside a warming tube with IVs and such. And I cried. I cried a lot. It was such a painful time for both my parents, but my dad especially. He felt guilty that the bird he'd encouraged to hang around the house had damaged his little girl. Then there was the time when someone let off fireworks under the bleachers at an Air Force football game and I came apart. My dad went and chased down those kids and gave them a piece of his mind. My dad was my protector. My hero.

There were lots of times when my dad had stepped up, taken my hand, and made everything all right. But he was older now, and so was I. He had a wife who needed day-to-day care due to chronic emphysema. He didn't have much left in the tank. He just couldn't carry the load of what I needed to tell him. I wished that Mike had never said anything. But that would not be fair either. So I gave him the short version. And he hugged me and gave me as much of himself as he could. And I was thankful for that.

Mom and Me

I NEEDED TO SPEND SOME TIME with my mom on my visit as well. She had been living in the memory care facility for about a year now. It was still hard to accept that we were losing her to dementia. In fact, it was hard to believe she was even at the point of needing a memory care facility. She had no other physical limitations and was, at least in her mind, ready for the golden age of retirement. We had convinced her to move in with my brother until we could find a suitable place for her. She thought that meant a home where she could have her freedom and independence once again. But that never happened.

The day we went to her doctor's office and he performed a basic memory test was so hard. Here was my mother, with her red-tinted hair, capris, Maui T-shirt, and turtle earrings, telling the doctor she didn't know if it was morning or night. She didn't remember the last time she ate, or if she was hungry. She did not know the month, not even the season. He ticked off about twenty questions, and at almost every turn, she just looked at us and shrugged her shoulders. No answer. She didn't even take a stab at them. It was painful for me and for her doctor. He had grown to love my mother and was a very compassionate man. But as someone who sat on the board for dementia-related diseases, he had given his fair share of these tests. And none of them were easy for anyone.

I am grateful to say that I am a lot like my mom. I do my best to see the glass as half full and believe in the power of a positive attitude. She certainly did so the day I moved her to the memory care center. She had been putting her foot down and saying she did not want to move to "that place"—even though she had toured "that place" a year earlier and found it to be quite to her liking. But a year can make a world of difference. Her ability to reason had dropped dramatically, as well as her ability to understand. I guess if I felt that someone wanted to convince me to move somewhere that I just couldn't quite understand, I would say no too. But she wasn't happy at my brother's house either. So we had all come together to make the decision for her to move to a home. And even though she would tell us no, we knew we had to do it. Down to the final day when it was time for her to move in, she still said no. In the final hours, I asked her if she wanted to run some errands with me, and she said, "Sure." My mom loved running errands. But instead of running errands, we drove directly to the home. I had no idea what to expect when we got there, but it was my only choice. I certainly expected a bit of a challenge on her end. But in the twenty minutes it took to drive there, her mind had cleared, and soon she stepped out of the car and into the welcoming hands of the staff at Oakdale. It seemed that she had suddenly made the decision to move there on her own accord, and she hoped we would all understand. She told me, "You know I love your brother, but I just needed my own place." God bless her.

I stayed with her and helped her to get settled in. We toured the home and then sat in the dining room while the staff offered snacks and drinks. It was almost as though Mom viewed the other residents as needy, lonely people she was suddenly there to help. She didn't see herself as a peer of the others. She would smile and wink at me as she went to help someone pull out a chair or put on their sweater; she seemed genuinely appreciative of her new duties. It was fascinating to watch her in action. Leaving her that day was hard, but my mom had shown me what she had always shown me: to keep your chin up no matter how hard life gets. But it wasn't until that moment that I understood it was not her good upbringing that gave her this gift; it was her spirit.

Going to see my mom on this trip brought up a lot of feelings for me. With regard to her own state of well-being, she was in a good place. She was engaging in all the activities. Once when I called to speak with her, the staff told me she was at happy hour! She had gained some weight and looked really good. Although her mind was continuing to fade, as a whole, she was in a good place. I walked into the room where she was doing her crafts, and she smiled at me and hugged me. Communication was becoming difficult, as she would struggle to find the words. But Mom had such expression in her eyes, and with the words she could get out, I was able to follow along.

What I found to be hard was that I was facing something really scary and unknown for the first time in my life, and I couldn't talk to my mom about it. I told her what was going on, the short version, and she just looked at me and smiled. On that particular day, I could have been reading an article from *Ladies' Home Journal* and she would have just looked at me and smiled. My heart sank. It wasn't that I had any expectations, because I had trained myself not to have expectations. But it was the reality of the space between us, the lifetime of love this woman had given me. I knew she would want to be concerned and she would want to hold me. I longed for that. But the message I sent to her got garbled up in the tangle of webs in her mind. And all she ended up with was something from *Ladies' Home Journal*. I felt that familiar lump in my throat, and my eyes filled. I smiled at her and laughed at the silliness of my even trying to tell her the news. I scolded myself for even telling her. But I felt that if I had put it out there in the universe for her to hear, maybe, somehow, she would know. And I believed that even if her response was complacent, maybe, just maybe, she heard me. I needed her to hear me.

All this time, I had been living in some sort of state of denial about my mom. I was good at pushing aside things that hurt, and had a strong résumé of doing so.

But there were cracks in my system, and as I knew from the past, this could all come tumbling in on me when I least expected it. I just couldn't figure out where the time had gone. How had she grown into this person so suddenly? It was only one year ago that we could talk and still understand each other. Had she known then what fate awaited her?

The reality of where my mom stood cast a shadow on me now. What kind of future was I facing? What would become of my body? Would I know it was going to happen? Would I have time to prepare? Or would MS sneak up on me as dementia had done to my mom? Time, so much time. Yet not enough time. Would I have the time to do the things I wanted to do in my life? Or would I be robbed of it? How many years did I have left? What would I do with them? It all caved in on me, one terrible scenario after another, like rocks sliding from a hillside. Once one comes down, more are sure to follow. I felt weak and scared. And I counted the hours before I could fly back to Cabo, stick my head back in the sand, and wait for my appointment in December.

More Waiting

BACK HOME IN CABO NOW, I was finding my space to breathe again. But as the saying goes, "once a bell has been rung, you can't unring it". The visit to San Diego had opened my eyes and my heart. I started to feel what it might be like to be a burden to those I love. I had seen the look in my father's eyes. And then there was the lack of anything from my mom, and the cruel reality of how life can be stolen from me when I least expect it. I did my best to put it all aside. But it had taken on a life of its own, like a wicked stepsister who was there to pester me all the time—except my new alter ego was one of shame, fear, and resentment.

The tools I needed so desperately at that time were not available at the hardware store—tools like the love of friends, family, and a job that brings fulfillment. I was being horrible to Keith. My fear and anger turned into a dislike for our life situation. I hadn't signed up for living in a Third World country, I would tell him. I felt trapped and turned my ugly side towards him. Sometimes we take crap from the ones we love because we are the only people they can vent their frustrations on. That was my sweet husband. He did whatever he could to help me find peace. He offered to move me to the States if it would make me happy. I knew that would only perpetuate conflict, and I knew what I was doing was wrong. I just didn't know what to do about it. Each day that I wasn't doing something engaging with my mind, body, or spirit felt like a complete waste. How many more days would I have? Would I wake up blind one morning and have that be the end of it? I wanted to go; I wanted to do. Unfortunately, "going and doing" was not the thing for me in Cabo. But above all, I wanted to ride.

Horses and Me

HORSES HAVE ALWAYS BEEN IN MY SOUL, as far back as I can remember. I don't really know when I fell in love with horses, that time when my heart made a leaping bound into a world where there was no turning back, a love affair that seemed to have been laid out for me one small stepping stone at a time. It was no different than any other love. I was helpless to its calling, and in the end, I would go to great lengths to protect it. And with such love comes heartbreak.

Perhaps it was when I took my first riding lesson. I was four or five years old, and we were living in Germany. My dad was in the Air Force, and we were stationed overseas. He and my mom wanted to give us a dose of real life living abroad, so they chose to live off base in the rolling hills of the countryside. Next to our home was a dairy farm. My mom would take us for outings to feed the cows. There was a unique smell at the dairy. It was like a big cauldron of earth, straw, and manure mixed with the hot breath of a milking cow—and I absolutely loved it.

Next to the dairy was a stable for horses. My mom had started to take riding lessons while my brothers were in school. I wasn't old enough for school yet, so I got to tag along and watch from the sidelines.

The barn was a gigantic place for a child my age. It had stall after stall of huge warmbloods and jumping stock breeds behind metal sliding gates. The steel rails along the front of the stalls were big enough for the horses to stick their noses out, just enough to get a pet and a carrot. My mom would put my small hand in hers and lay it flat so that they could take the carrot. I always giggled at the feeling of their muzzles and whiskers as they nosed along my small hand.

On the weekends, my dad and my brothers would also come with us for Mom's lesson. As it turned out, my dad was terrified of the big animals. When we would walk the stalls to give them treats, my dad would say, "Watch out, that one has his ears back. He's going to bite you!" I just couldn't fathom that and never heeded his warnings. My mom would tell him to shush, and we'd all laugh. But inside me, something had sprouted. I felt keenly aware that these magnificent animals were gentle and trusting beyond even my father's own imagination.

It wasn't long before my mom felt that I should be taking lessons too. And to my complete surprise, my dad went along with it. He was such a good read, and he knew this was something important to my mom and to me. His two girls, how could he resist?

There were no fully outfitted, saddled horses at the learning center. In Germany, we learned by only using a thin pad and a vaulting girth. This is a type of girth that goes around the belly of the horse and up and over the withers, with handles and loops in different locations. There are no stirrups, and the rider does not use reins. A trainer guides the horse in large circles using a lunge line. All of these things are meant to bring the horse and rider into as close a contact as possible, with just enough stability to make it safe and secure.

From what I can remember at that young age, it was an incredible experience, riding high on the back of this large animal, holding my arms out to the front and sides as he trotted in circles. My little body began to mold and bend naturally to the body of the big horse. It was such a thrill, but also such a natural fit for me. I can only imagine how the horse felt, a small butterfly squirming about on top of his back. I learned to find my balance by pushing forward, sideways, and back until I settled in. And that big horse trusted that I would soon learn to connect, and I did.

I learned to turn my body full circle while cantering. Other times, I would sit up on top of him with my shins resting on the sides of his warm and soft flesh, with my arms held forward as if we were charging the stars. We walked, we trotted, and we cantered, round and round in circles. It was as if I were entranced with each turn, each roll of his back. The warmth of his body and the steam that came off his breath when we stopped to rest reassured me that this animal held me safely and calmly in his care. What a magical experience—I wanted it to last forever.

Divorce

"SOMETIME MOMMIES AND DADDIES love their children but they don't know how to love each other anymore." These were the words my mom spoke to us as we loaded the car headed for the airport. We were bound for the US that day—four tickets, not five. My dad would not be coming. He was staying. I was six years old now, and these words she spoke didn't quite translate to me. But I could see through the looks on my brothers' faces that they had a profound meaning and something was about to go terribly off-kilter.

At the airport, my father carried me on his shoulders through the airport. I was a gangly young girl who had a mad crush on her dad. He'd left us before, to go serve our country in Korea and other parts of the world. But he always returned. This time, we were the ones leaving, and it had a completely different feeling to me. My mom later told me that I cried and held on to my father with all my might—I made a big scene, and people watched and wondered. And her heart broke all the more knowing our family would never be the same.

We arrived in San Diego in the springtime. My mom, my two older brothers, and I moved in with my grandparents for a few months until Mom could get on her feet. We enrolled in a new school, and life started over.

Mom eventually landed a job, and we moved into our own apartment. She worked Monday through Friday, nine to five. We did what other latchkey kids did at the time, which was to go to school, walk home, and open the door, and then all hell would break loose. Being the youngest of three, with two bullheaded brothers, I learned to stay out of the way.

It was strange and different for us to suddenly have all this freedom. Up until this point, we'd been so lucky to have our mom at our beck and call. She was always there for us. And suddenly now, she wasn't.

My mother was a pretty woman with a slender build, warm brown eyes, and great legs. Her overbite gave her a bigger-than-life smile, and she had a witty personality to match. I was amazed at how fast she could transform from a housewife to a secretary of the seventies. She took her new role as the head of household with great ease, and at no point did we feel lost. Money was tight and she stretched each dollar, but we didn't worry about the next day. We felt safe, loved, and nurtured. Sometimes all she could offer up at the end of the day was a heaping stack of hotcakes fresh off the griddle. In her polyester dress and with a cigarette in her hand, she was every bit the family martyr we needed, and we all believed in her. She had a way of making everything an adventure. To this day, I have never met a pancake I didn't like.

Things went on like this for several months, and then Mom began dating Phil, a man she worked with at the time. He was a gentle man with a fun personality. They seemed to enjoy each other. His children would join us on the weekends sometimes. It was a new beginning, and Mom seemed happy. Things were falling into place, and even though I missed my dad dearly, our new life was a great distraction from that.

Mom had recently reconnected with her cousin Dottie. Word had it that Aunt Dottie and her family lived out in the countryside and had a small farm, including horses. And Aunt Dottie had a daughter the exact same age as me. "Her name is Katrina," my mom told me. "She rides horses." That was all I needed to hear.

More Horses

ONE SATURDAY MORNING, we were going to visit Aunt Dottie. Mom and Phil packed us up in the truck and we were off. My brothers and I loved going on road trips. Riding in the back of a pickup truck with the wind in our hair and the sound and feel of the road beside us was such a rush. We'd all squeeze behind the cab of the truck and hold our jackets tight. We played a game of "I called it," which meant whatever we each saw along the way that we dreamed of owning, we called it. It was all a matter of who could claim the most and the best the fastest. By the end of the hour-long ride through the winding country roads, we had all amassed more cars, houses, and boats than our little brains could handle. I was the only one claiming horses, so I was by far the richest in the world.

As we slowed to pull off the road and onto the long dirt driveway, I could see what looked like a ranch house in the distance. The home sat up high on a ridge. And below the house was a beautiful white-fenced arena. Beyond the white fencing were corrals, and inside those corrals were the horses.

We were first greeted by barks and wags of the family German Shepherd, named ten-four. Soon after, Aunt Dottie and the others came out to welcome us as well. Dottie's son, Jeff, had rounded up my brothers, and they ran off shouting something about BB gun practice. Mom and Phil were exchanging pleasantries with Aunt Dottie and Uncle Ron when, out of the corner of my eye, I spotted a blonde girl about my age. She was coming towards us up a dirt trail from the area below. And behind her was a shiny chocolate-colored pony with a shaggy forelock, mane, and tail. She had been freshly groomed and had a lilac-colored bow in her tail—the same color as the bow in the blonde girl's hair.

She came to us on the grassy knoll, and Dottie introduced her as my cousin Katrina. She had a strong voice and a pleasant personality, and she said rather quickly, "Hi! Mom says you're my cousin and you're from Germany. What'd you do in Germany? This is my pony, Denise. You can ride her if you want. Want to ride her?"

I can't think of too many people in my life who, by meeting in a chance encounter, have altered the way my life would play out. And I certainly didn't know it in that moment, but this was one of those people and one of those chance encounters. Katrina and I went on to become sisters, not cousins. We grew, we fought, and we loved horses—first her horses and then, as time went on, our own horses. We were two kindred spirits who just happened to be born into the same family.

Not long after that, Mom and Phil decided that living in separate places was a waste of time. They rented a small three-bedroom ranch home on about an acre in what I would describe as a new rural suburban area. It was a warm house that sat back off the street with a flat, fenced, square acre lot just perfect for stretching our wings. The area of town had small mini-ranches sprinkled about, and on our first drive by to see our new home, I envisioned corrals in the back of that yard. Similar to how some people see money signs flashing before their eyes when playing the lotto or gambling, I dreamed of white railings and shiny metal feeders. I smelled the hay and the manure, and wondered what the horses who would live in these corrals would look like. I let my imagination run free.

The universe works in mysterious ways, and with all my prayers wrapped up in one little package, it must not have been too difficult to answer. Mom and Phil grew increasingly closer and decided it was time to try their hand at horsemanship. And as it turned out, Aunt Dottie already had a perfect opportunity for us: a dappled buckskin mare with a white flaxen mane and tail. Yvette was a beautiful horse in body and spirit, and with Aunt Dottie's help, she came home to us.

The day for our new horse to arrive had come, and I was all in stitches. I did all that I could to keep myself occupied, but time crept ever so slowly. Finally, with yet another glance down the drive, I could see Aunt Dottie's red four-door pickup truck towing her white two-horse trailer.

Yvette's black tail with white frosting stuck out the back, and although she stomped a few times, she was quiet in the trailer. The thought of her passing through the same winding hills and roads that we had traveled to her old house brought a smile to my face. Had she seen the ranches I had claimed for myself in our game of "I called it"? Was there something out there that she wanted to call her own? Maybe a young girl, perhaps, who only wanted to love and care for a horse like her? Maybe she had called that. Maybe she had claimed me. But Yvette was going to be my mom's horse, which meant the rest of us had to stand in line for visitation rights.

She backed slowly out of the trailer, looking every bit as pretty as I remembered. While spending time at the ranch with Katrina, I had already come to know Yvette. We had taken photos of her on our last visit, when the arrangements were made for her to come to our home. I had kept one of the Polaroids in my room and had long since been studying every inch of her. I had even taken the photo to school to share with my class during show-and-tell. I was such a shy child that I rarely shared anything. But that morning, all my fears and angst of speaking in front of class melted away. In my mind, I was standing beside her and she was in the room with me. I drew strength and courage from just thinking of her. I'd had an important announcement to make, and surely the fact that we had a horse in the family was newsworthy.

Mom led Yvette around the property while we tagged along, giggling with excitement. She was wearing a hunter-green halter and seemed so elegant to me. She walked cautiously but was so trusting in her leader that it felt like she'd surely done this before. Mom soon took her to her corral, removed her halter, and set her free.

The neighbors had an apricot tree that was full of ripe fruit. It hung over the fence just enough that it dropped several ripe apricots along the fence and into her corral. I watched as she walked over to investigate. As she slowly collected them in her soft muzzle, she peeled away the fresh fruit and then spat out the pits. Her tail whisking gently back and forth, she was happy. And with each licking of the lips and each sigh, snort, and deep breath, she showed me this was the right home for her.

The air was warm, and the ground had started to cool with the setting sun. An auburn cast of sunlight lay across the horizon and landed on her back. The golden dapples weaved together like bubbles reaching up to the sky. I sat cross-legged on the ground, looking up at her and trying to count them. One, twelve, twenty—there were just so many of those beautiful dapples. I knew I counted some of them more than once, but I didn't mind. And as the sky grew darker, I found myself staring into her wide-set eyes—deep brown pools of unimaginable glory. Those beautiful eyes looked deep into my soul and spoke words of promise.

Life settled into a wonderful new rhythm. Before long, Mom and Phil had gotten married and our mini-ranch grew with the addition of dogs, cats, goats, and an ornery pony named Shadow. Shadow was a gun-steel gray Shetland with a light crimson mane and tail that were as puffy as cotton candy. But sweet she was not, and after a couple of incidents of her running away with me, and me ditching her for the ground, it was decided that she should move on to another family. I continued to ride Yvette, and one would think I was sad to lose Shadow, but she and I never really bonded. There was coldness in her eyes that I trusted to mean she was done with kids plunking along on her. And I knew then that I wasn't one to question it. Shadow had spoken, and we heeded her warnings.

Soon after this, there was a new mare in our family. Melody was a curvy gray Arabian with big bones and a friendly face. It was especially exciting when Melody arrived, because she was in foal.

Melody was a specimen. She stood tall and square, and seemed larger in body and personality than Yvette. If Melody was a person, I would say she reminded me of Marilyn Monroe. She had a quiet personality and was very eager to please, so we all fell in love with her. Quickly she grew and grew, and after months of waiting, it was time for her to welcome her young one into the world. I was older now, and the act of birthing was of interest to me. Just after dark on a hot summer night, she began her pacing. First she walked and swayed before lying down in the fresh nest of straw and then got back up again. She walked to the corner of the stall and stood with her butt up against the rails and then went back over to the straw again. This time, she lay down and began to push.

Mom and Phil were in the stall with her, and the rest of us were lined up against the railing. Before long, I could hear my mom squeal with excitement that she could see the hooves. Then with a sudden and quick push came the muzzle, followed by the rest of the torso. In a sack of shiny blue-looking goo was a black blob. Melody immediately pushed herself up and was quick to start licking and nuzzling her foal. I looked at my mom and could feel her tears running down her cheeks. Happy tears. Mom took a towel and ran it over the foal's body to help clean her up. She slowly rubbed her hands over the foal, long gentle strokes that were to leave the baby with a familiarity of us humans. Imprinting.

The black blob shook and bobbled around in the straw. Melody finished nuzzling her baby. My parents determined that we had a baby girl. She was as dark as a cup of rich brewed coffee, with a tall white sock on her back leg and a crooked thin blaze running down her face. Within an hour, she was standing, and soon after, she was nursing. It was like the scene from *Bambi* where he was on ice, with all four legs going every which way. Each step forward took considerable balance and determination. And then she toppled over only once, quickly gained her footing, and was back up standing once again.

We all stood in wonder as we witnessed this new life find her way. It was incredible how fast she went from the black blob to a dry furry baby, walking and nursing and even letting out a whinny to let her mother know she was well. It was nature's way of counting all her fingers and toes. Mother Melody knew that she had one healthy baby girl on her hands. And baby knew that in the safety of her new home, she didn't need to be in such a hurry. In the wild, horses need to be able to move within hours of birth—after all, they are prey animals, and baby horses are the weakest link. But Melody and baby walked the stall in short strides. Baby girl stayed as close to her mother's side as physically possible. And with one final lick of baby's forehead, Melody closed her eyes and rested. It had been a big night.

Months went on, and soon we had a name for baby girl. I was given the opportunity to name her, and I decided Mandy was a perfect fit. Melody and Mandy spent their days together in the paddock. It was such fun to watch them as Mandy grew and experienced all the pleasures of life on the farm—the playful antics of a young horse and the steady support of her loving mother. In some ways, I felt as if Mandy and I had something in common. We were both young, and growing and changing too fast for our own good. Like her, I wanted to run like the wind. I dreamed of being on her back, running fearlessly through tall grass and over fences. I'd see myself with my arms held apart, riding bareback with just a thin blanket between us to hold us together. I dreamed, and I watched, and I waited.

Mandy turned a year old, and for my eleventh

birthday, she was officially given to me. I was so surprised. My mom had made a picture book of our first year together, and inside the book, she wrote "For your 11th Birthday, your very own Mandy." I was ecstatic, and at the same time, I felt my heart sink a little. Mandy was just a year old. She was an Arabian, and this meant that she needed more time than other horses before I could ride her. As much as I was thrilled and my heart was full, I felt I had waited long enough. Waiting two more years for her to be broke and properly trained before I could ride her seemed like an eternity. My parents' gift was an immeasurable act of love. But I had riding to do, and if it meant riding another horse before Mandy was ready, then so be it.

The Sunday paper had always been a piece of entertainment for our family. Of course news articles and the Sunday comics were popular. I particularly loved looking through the livestock and animals section of the classifieds. We lived in a rural town, so there were always interesting finds in the classifieds. And there were always a few horses or ponies for sale too. As much as I adored baby Mandy, I was eleven years old and felt I would die before she grew old enough for me to ride. I ached to have a horse I could ride from dawn to dusk. And even though I knew I was fortunate to have had Mandy as a gift, I also knew that some tactical gentle persuasion wouldn't hurt. So each week as the family nonchalantly looked over the paper, I scanned the livestock section for any possible leads on a riding horse.

I thought I was building a solid case with my steady persistence and subtle pouting. I knew never to push too hard. I continued to scan the weekly classifieds. We also went to the auction on occasion. I would waste not a single second as we parked before I'd jump out the door of the truck and run to the corrals that held the livestock. A few months of this went by, and I began to lose hope. I knew I should be happy with Mandy. And I was; I loved her. But deep down inside, something inside me was calling "You go, girl." I was meant to be on the back of a horse.

As timing would have it, my persistence was about to pay off. Phil had started to gain sympathy towards my cause. I would catch him reading the classifieds in hiding so that my mother wouldn't see him. When I talked about how much fun I would have and what hundreds of chores I would perform if only I could get a horse of my own, I would see Phil's mouth crack a smile and he'd give me a wink over his reading glasses. My mom, on the other hand, proved to be a hard nut to crack. But Phil had a big heart, and he knew how much this would mean to me. He became my ally, the only person rooting for my team. Suddenly I wasn't feeling so defeated.

One weekend, I woke up and strolled into the kitchen for breakfast like I always did. Everyone was off doing something, and as I sat and ate my cereal, Phil walked up behind me. He was holding his cup of coffee in one hand, and in the other, he held the classifieds. Folded into threes, it was a piece of paper big enough to swat a fly. And as I looked at it, I could see a large red circle around one ad. He looked at me with a half-cocked grin and plunked it down in front of me. And then he walked away.

The listing in the classifieds was simple. People paid by the word in those days, and this horse was worth no more than the minimum allotment. The description was as follows: "9-year-old Hackney Welsh Pony, 13.1 hands,

Bay, white sock, needs intermediate rider. $200." And then it was followed by a local phone number. Those seven numbers looked like a winning lottery ticket to me. And they held the key to fulfilling my dream.

I later heard my mom and Phil talking on the patio. Soon afterwards, my mom came inside and went to make a phone call. She asked the person on the other end a few questions. How long have you had him? Why are you selling him? Is he an easy keeper? It felt like an eternity as I held my breath. I was still playing dumb, and as long as I kept my mouth shut, things seemed to be going in the right direction. But my patience was growing thin. Just as I was building up my courage to ask her about all of this, Mom hung up the phone, turned to me, and said, "Get yourself ready. We're going to look at a horse."

His name was Dandy, and he lived two miles away from us on the other side of the Rocky Home Dairy. He belonged to a young girl about my age. Her name was Janet, and she and I went to the same school. Her parents had bought him for her to run barrels. He had been a solid competitor but, to their surprise, had grown ring shy. This happens when a horse is asked to perform the same duty over and over again without enough reward or outside stimulation. He came to her this way, and though she was patient with him, she just never could get him to walk into the ring. Other than this, they described him as a perfect riding companion. But they were honest and did not want him to pass on to another little girl to be disappointed. I had no interest in riding for show. My goals were quite different. I was looking for a friend, my own riding buddy and companion, someone to share in my adventures.

Dandy was a sight for sore eyes. He stood quietly as I ran my eyes over his beautiful brown body. His mane had been trimmed and grew to stand three inches high, and he had a broad, raised nose, which all reminded me of a picture I had seen of Roman horses. They tacked him up, and we went for a ride around their property. I felt strong and confident on his back. Clearly he felt relaxed with me. We walked in circles, and I could feel his breath. With each movement, we folded a little more into each other, and soon it was hard to tell where he ended and I began. Although I could hear small talk between the others, I could also feel my mom's eyes on me, observing us from afar. We rounded the corner once more, and her eyes met mine. They were soft and round and wet. She smiled and shrugged, and it was then that I knew he was the one for me—and that he was coming home.

The sun was setting, and the dust from the ring where we had ridden was low. My mom and Phil bid farewell to Janet and her parents. It was decided that I would ride Dandy home and we would return the bridle and bareback pad to them the following morning. We started off towards home. Mom and Phil drove slowly behind us for a short while. But they soon grew bored and hollered out the window that they would see me at home. And suddenly, there I was, poking along Garden Road atop my pony. My very own pony. The pony I'd dreamed about and wished for with every one of my eleven-year-old limbs. With each step, my legs dangled next to his warm, big, brown body. I felt the whole world opening up before us. I had the friend I'd always dreamed of.

The friendship I shared with Dandy was magical, a perfect match made in heaven. We fit together like two peas in a pod, and that first summer was full of adventure and surprise. Janet had gotten a new horse, and together we set out each day to cover new ground with our trusted steeds. We did our best to keep things interesting. Sometimes, we would find ourselves at the lake, and with a cue from me, we would run as fast as we could around the lake. Once we arrived on the other side, we would find a large shade tree and let the reins fall to the ground so they could graze the green grass, and then we would lie back and talk and giggle, both dressed in shorts, rainbow T-shirts, and slip-on tennis shoes. Our horses wore nothing more than a cotton bareback pad and bridles.

Other times, we would take the horses into the lake and swim with them. Janet had more experience with this than I did, and I let her show me the way. Soon Dandy and I were afloat, his head above water and his back holding me up gently as his strong legs pulled us through the water. I held on to the bareback pad and floated along, enjoying the ride. Oh, the horses loved that. We always had a few coins in our pockets, and on the way home, we often rode our horses through the drive-through at Jack in the Box to buy some fries. Then we'd sit in the shade and share them, with the horses, of course. We rode our horses to Sunday school, after school, and anytime there wasn't school. The lessons we learned outside the classroom were priceless.

One Sunday, I followed Janet to a show. And even though I'd been warned that Dandy would not go into an arena, we tried our hand at barrel racing. It turned out that he'd gotten over his fear and resistance to the ring, and together we rode ourselves into the senior division. It wasn't long before the walls of my bedroom were draped in ribbons of all colors. Our friendship had broken down the boundaries that had held him back. And his confidence built me up. It was all so wonderful, just a kid and her horse.

Horses and Healing

THROUGHOUT ALL THE YEARS in between my childhood and my adulthood, there were other horses. Whether it was a friend who needed someone to ride their horse or even Aunt Dottie's horses, I had always managed to keep one foot in the door with them and continued to dream of having a horse again one day. The lessons of the heart horses gave me never left me and were never replaced by a new love. And here I was, facing something so daunting, so scary, that the thought of never being able to ride again only made me want it more. So I dreamt of riding. I knew the feel of a horse, and their strength was healing. On the back of a horse, I felt no fear or anxiety. I had ridden off into the sunset on many occasions in my life, and even though I had to turn around and come home, I was always better for it.

Ronald Reagan once said, "There is nothing better for the inside of a man than the outside of a horse." I could not agree more. But in Cabo, you don't just open the phone book and find a riding stable to visit or look in the classifieds for what ails you. Life is not lived in black and white; there are many shades in between. And oftentimes in Cabo, you don't find what you are looking for; you have to wait for it to find you.

It was mid-October now, and I decided that I needed to talk to my therapist. Maybe some Skype sessions with my counselor back in Park City would give me the clarity and direction that I was so desperately seeking. My husband was not one for shrinks, but he loved me and knew that if I was asking about this, then there was a darn good reason for it.

I set up a session with Lana. She was the person I had gone to when I needed someone to talk to before we made the move to Mexico. I'd been experiencing anxiety over the move and what lay ahead for us. It had taken a lot for me to adjust to the move to Park City, and then four years later, I'd finally found my place and we were up and leaving for Mexico.

There were other issues that lay under the surface as well. Like a scratch and sniff, all it took was a little digging and she had touched on a subject that I had worked hard to move past. The four years it took to get my balance in Park City were especially hard because the very day we had arrived to start our new life, my ex-husband had decided to end his. At the very moment I landed in my new home, a phone call was all it took to unhinge any plan of happiness and new beginnings. A relationship that had lasted seventeen years had been turned to dust on that fall day in October. And when Lana began her soft yet thorough assessment of me, it became obvious that something had burned fast and hard on my soul.

And with all the efforts I had taken to snuff it out, there were scars that hadn't healed.

Patrick

PATRICK AND I MET when I was celebrating my twenty-first birthday. He was a cute boy and he had a strong personality, but underneath, there was a truthful gentleness. We dated, and then five years later, we married. I had all the hopes for a white-picket-fence life: a house, a yellow Labrador, and children. But, as it is with life, the white picket fence can be elusive. It's a mirage. You might see just enough of it to believe it to be true, but when you reach for it, it does not exist. Our marriage survived in this state for twelve years.

There was a separation in our seventh year of marriage, at which point we did one year of marriage counseling. Each week, we would go and sit with our therapist for an hour. After five more years of living the mirage, I was done. I was tired of living in a marriage of loneliness and isolation. Patrick was a people person, and in his world, he needed to be constantly involved with people, and sports, and business. I'm convinced it was a way to protect himself from the underlying issues of his mental illness. If he stayed busy, stayed involved and active, he could navigate his life. Unfortunately for me, it meant being alone a lot, being at the bottom of the list. My family, the things that were important to me, were not enough to sustain his need for survival. He tried; I tried. Eventually I woke up to the fact that my life, our marriage, was the mirage. The white picket fence evaded me still.

And so we divorced. I tried to convince him to see his doctor. I knew he was hurting and his mental state was vulnerable. I knew the fragile side of him. We never spoke of it, but it's impossible to live under the same roof as someone and not know they are suffering. He would never agree to get help. He would tell me that drugs were not for him. He needed to be whatever raw version of himself that he was. And he would not accept taking medication that would alter his personality—even if it meant saving his life. This was his choice.

The day I moved out, I told him I had made an appointment for him with his doctor. When I followed up a week later, they told me he'd been in but there was no mention of how serious his situation was. His sisters tried to intervene and get him help, but he evaded that intervention too. A soul comes into this world alone and goes out alone—that's what he would tell me. The choice was his. And my choice to leave was mine. I could say, from the depths of my heart, I knew something might happen to him—that he might hurt himself. But I could no longer stay in that place because of this. My leaving meant I had to accept this fact but not accept the responsibility. I was not responsible.

The divorce papers were signed. I had taken the house in Park City as part of our separation of assets. Patrick had kept the house in San Diego. It had been a long and drawn-out situation, one in which Patrick disappeared for months and months, only to surface again and finally sign the divorce papers.

Keith and I had been dating, and with all the drama and hurt that comes with divorce, I needed to get away from San Diego. So I suggested to him that we move to Park City for the winter. A fresh start would be good for me, and in Park City, Keith and I could work on starting a new life. We were in love. It was the kind of love that I had never experienced before. At age thirty-eight, I felt like I was truly starting over. I felt fortunate to have this opportunity. But I also knew leaving would come at a price: my entire life, my family, my job, and my friends. My dog, Roy, was to stay with Patrick. He said he felt isolated and alone, and wanted to keep him. That was a gut-wrenching decision. But I felt Roy had a place in all of this. I accepted that sometimes I needed to let the ones I love go. I had to set him free. And if he was meant to come back to me, he would.

I knew that Keith and I needed a new, healthy space to grow. Our family and our friends would be there for us in San Diego. We would go to Park City and start over. After all the hurt and anxiety of those months during the long, drawn-out divorce, I felt like now was my time to fly. Little did I know, I would be grounded before I ever took off.

The Call

KEITH AND I LEFT SAN DIEGO on October 17. We were driving our separate cars so that we could get them there at the same time. After making it to Mesquite, Nevada, and staying over at the Best Western, we woke up to a gorgeous fall morning. It was cool and crisp outside. The Weather Channel showed there was snow on the Parley's Canyon, the long canyon highway that leads from Salt Lake to Park City. I felt so calm that morning. My mind was quiet and my nerves were still. The sight of snow made us giddy inside. We were on our way to our new life and a winter we would never forget. I felt so safe and happy. It was as if all the miles between San Diego and Mesquite, Nevada, and the closing of that day into a new one, had turned me around completely. The heavy load I had been carrying with me had been left along the road somewhere, out in the desert with all the other useless rocks. My emotional baggage was lifted, and I felt so hopeful.

Keith and I left for Park City around nine thirty that morning. Thirty minutes into the drive, we started up a beautiful, rocky mountain gorge, which was spectacular. While winding around between huge rock formations, it was hard not to be touched by the beauty. As I let my mind wander, I came to this one thought that struck me. It was a feeling of infinity, the feeling that what happens on this earth is only the beginning. I felt a big lift with the sudden knowing that whatever hurt had been left unhealed in my past would be washed away and that no matter what lay ahead in Patrick's life, I would see him in heaven someday. He would be whole and healed, and there would be no pain. And my life ahead would be full and long and new, but in infinity, all things are healed. That was a powerful feeling for me. So with that thought, I drove through the Virgin River Gorge, and between nine thirty and ten thirty in the morning, I felt lighter still without the load I had carried. And as I crested the valley to drive into the high desert, I felt transformed, as if an angel had carried me through.

Six hours later, we pulled into our new home. Keith's cat, Kitty, greeted us at the door. We had driven her, and the first load of our things, out ten days prior. She was happy to see us and took us on a tour of her new home. The sun was setting and filled the living room with a golden light. We opened a split of champagne and said "cheers" to each other for making it to this new place—to what lay ahead, to our love, and to the simple things that a new relationship can hope for. Keith had been there for me in ways my family and friends were not. He had been tested right out of the gate with all the drama I endured during the divorce. I had always felt guilty for him having so much to deal with from the woman he fell in love with. But at this moment, it was all behind us. We could dedicate ourselves to each other now. I was so happy knowing he would no longer need to be a rock for me.

We went to dinner, and on our way home, my cell phone rang. I looked down at my phone and saw the caller ID. I looked at the phone and then looked at the road ahead. How quickly we were going off course. We were only three miles from home, but I wanted to keep driving. I wanted to turn around and run for the hills. Maybe if I threw my phone out the window, I could pretend this wasn't happening. Because once I saw who was calling me, I knew. I knew he had done it. I felt it in the deepest hollows of my heart. He was gone.

I told Keith the call was from Patrick's family, but I didn't tell him why. It would be wrong of me to assume such a thing, but I knew. And so when I called back and was told that on that morning, at ten fifteen, Patrick had succeeded in taking his own life, all I could do was scream. Scream and hang up the phone. The horror was unfolding for me now. I quickly called back, and we only spoke a few words. It was all I could do. There was nothing, absolutely nothing I could say. For so many years, I thought this day may come. I thought it was a possibility, but now it was real. Keith held me, and I cried and I cried. I made phone calls, paced our house full of boxes, and cried some more. We drank wine and unpacked, and then I cried even more. At one o'clock that morning, Keith turned to me and said, "You have to stop. You have to get a grip." And he was right. I had to make a choice: either go down the rathole of despair or accept this and keep my life moving forward.

The Aftermath

THE FOLLOWING MORNING, while I was standing in the closet and looking for something to wear, Keith brought me my phone. It was Matt, the man who had been the best man when Patrick and I got married. After some small talk, he said directly to me, "Christie, I need to tell you something; listen very closely. The lawyer who handled your divorce was called about Patrick's death. He said that you are the one who is responsible for his estate and for the handling of his funeral. Patrick did not make any other arrangements after you two signed your divorce papers, so by law, you're next of kin." And then he went on talking about how there would be a lot of decisions to make, and it would cost a lot of money, and I needed to come back to San Diego to handle these things, and so on.

There I was, with puffy eyes and in shock from learning of his death the previous day, and now I was responsible? For his funeral? For the house, his business, his stuff, his world? How could this possibly be happening? It was hard enough for me to find something suitable to wear in that very moment, and they wanted me to get on a plane and fly back to San Diego? To do this? I needed to get off the phone and think. I held my cell phone in my hand and looked at it. What an evil device this had turned into. My phone was now a cord that held me responsible for all that unfolded back in San Diego. I had no time to fall apart. While everyone else could, I had to hold it together to get through this. I felt sick, and weak, and confused.

I tried to explain to Keith, and he just looked at me in disbelief. Months into a relationship, we were about to be tested to the limit. My heart was shattered into pieces, but it had hope. And that hope was all tied to my future with Keith. How twisted and divided I felt. It was like two worlds were colliding inside me. My old life, which

I thought had been sealed with the signing of a divorce and a decision to move, was now a giant thunderstorm enveloping me and suffocating my future—Keith's and my future. But I knew I had to do the right thing. I knew that our relationship was about to be tested. And I hoped that in the end, we would pass and come back here, and we would start again.

That evening, as I lay in bed, trying to fall asleep, my mind raced. I had no more tears—there would be plenty of tears later. What I had was fear and anxiety that the loss of Patrick would forever change me, that somehow I was going to get lost in the grief and time would stop, leaving me trapped there in that horrible emotional place. I thought long and hard, and I made a promise to myself. I spoke out loud as if saying it instead of just thinking it would make me keep my word: "I promise that this moment will not define you, and you will not get stuck in this. You will keep moving through this no matter what." Those words were huge to me. They gave me clarity and a sense of courage. I knew deep down inside that this whole thing was about to get really hard, but somewhere out there, there would come a day—long after Patrick had been laid to rest—that I, too, would be able to put it all down and walk off to start again. It would come. I would get there. I promised.

The next morning, we boarded a plane for San Diego. There were eight days of planning a funeral while some of the worst wildfires to hit San Diego raged outside of town. In the end, on a clear and crisp October morning, close to five hundred people showed up to pay their respects to a man who had brought so much magic to their lives. Giving him the service and burial he wanted and deserved was hard on so many levels, but I look back and feel it was an honor. No longer as his wife but now as a friend, I felt honored to give this man the funeral he wanted with what was important to him.

Keith was there for me during this week too. He drove me around to appointments, waiting but not getting involved. I attended the services while he stayed with his family, out of the drama but only a phone call away. He was an ever-ready source of strength and support for me when I had no one else to turn to. He made sure I ate, kept me laughing when it was hard to smile, and allowed me to go through the process in my own way. We had no idea we'd end up in this place together, but here we were. And together we got through it.

Although my responsibilities continued into the coming months and years, I kept my promise to myself: Our life got back on track, and we moved on from it. The emotional healing took time too. There is no filing date to close down emotional healing. But as time went on, the gap closed and I grew into a new life, a wonderful life with Keith and a new understanding of marriage and relationships that I had not experienced before. Second chances rarely come, and I was so fortunate to get a second chance.

Asking for Help

BACK IN CABO, feeling like I was drowning with no-where to turn, I needed to get some help. Keith had been a constant form of stability as best he could, but I could feel myself tilting towards the fear and anxiousness of the unknown with my health and my life's direction. Reaching out to Lana seemed like the right thing to do. So after a quick email to her, we scheduled a session via Skype.

I ran down the list of what I had been dealing with recently, and Lana listened, asked questions, and gently probed me to divulge the real fearful issues at hand. She explained to me that it was perfectly normal—with all the change I'd experienced, and now the uncertainty—to feel the way I did. In talking to her, I expressed my desire to "just get on a horse and ride," to be able to gain strength in something familiar that had always empowered me. She encouraged me to stay positive and to look for those things in my daily life. I needed to harness a mindset of blessings, not curses. Was the glass half full or half empty? No matter how bleak life feels, there is always something to be thankful for. I knew it; I just needed to start focusing on those things.

Lana and I closed with some laughs, and some tears. I felt immensely lifted by her sincere words. I promised to follow through with the exercises she had set forth, and we set a time to talk again the following week.

Tomatoes and Friends

TWO DAYS LATER, I went with my friend Nicole to a Tomatoes luncheon. It was October, and all the snowbirds were returning to Cabo. I started to see them in the stores and restaurants, and expected quite a crowd for this luncheon.

Nicki and I sat at a table, and not long after, a friend of hers named Linda joined us. Linda then invited her friend Fran, and together with two other ladies, we had a nice table of six.

The usual greetings went around. I introduced myself, and we all got to chatting about this and that. The restaurant, La Pampa, is an Argentinian steak house, so we noshed on red wine and empanadas, olives, and tapenades.

As the afternoon wound down, I overheard Linda and Fran solidifying their plans for the following morning. Someone mentioned going riding, and I quickly grew intrigued and asked if they were going horseback riding. One of them answered, "Yes, we both keep our horses at a barn not far from here and are riding in the morning. There is another horse out at the barn, and he needs someone to give him some exercise. Would you like to join us?" I was beside myself with excitement and grabbed my pencil and paper to take down the details. I didn't ask any questions about what kind of horse he was, or what kind of riding we would do—there was an opening and I was going to take it. Linda gave me her phone number and told me to confirm with her. So as soon as I got to my car after leaving the restaurant, I called her to confirm. She gave me the directions, and soon I was smiling from ear to ear. I was going riding in the morning!

I got home and assembled my clothes for the morning. I rounded up some old tennis shoes, dug up a pair of blue jeans and a long-sleeved white shirt to keep the sun off me, and grabbed a hat, sunscreen, and a water bottle—and a handful of carrots for the mystery horse I would meet in the morning.

Meeting Milagro

THE NEXT MORNING, I hustled to get through the morning routine. I made breakfast in the usual fashion. Roy and I took a brisk walk, and I apologized to him for cutting our time short, but I had big plans that day. Keith was dressed in his work attire, and as we walked out to our cars together, he kissed me and wished me luck.

Jotted down on a piece of paper were the directions to the barn. Drive down the four-lane, make a U-turn at the Esperanza Resort, and then make a right turn onto the dirt road at the Modelorama factory. Drive up the dirt road past the school, and then look for the large wooden gate.

I parked my Jeep alongside the road, next to a few other dusty vehicles. As I approached the gate, I spotted a woman riding a black-and-white horse down the road towards us, a tall-framed gal with long, thick hair tied up in a bun, wearing a sunhat. As I entered the gate, Linda was there to greet me, and at the same time, the woman riding the black-and-white horse came up alongside us. She had been out on the trails already, and her horse was sweaty from the early-morning exercise. She looked at me and asked without hesitation if I was there to ride Milagro. I looked at Linda since I didn't know the name of the horse yet, but she confirmed to the woman that I was the person she had met and invited out to ride. This woman looked strangely familiar to me, and she was sizing me up just the same, as if she felt I was familiar too. I don't know who said it first, but we both laughed when we figured out that we had met the prior year at the Dressed to the K9's party. I told her my name, and she gave me hers: Elizabeth. Linda explained that Elizabeth was Milagro's mom and that she had rescued him.

It was a quick walk from the front of the property to the barn area, and as the three of us walked towards the barn, I was taking everything in. Fran was riding in the arena to the right of us, and we were passing stalls of horses to the left. The barn was built out of brick, so as we walked by, I could not see the entire row of horses, only each one as we passed their stall. Suddenly Elizabeth stopped in front of one of the stalls. A large steel door was used for the gate. I had to peer over the top to see the horse inside.

Elizabeth made quick introductions: "Here he is. This is Milagro." And as I looked over the gate at the mystery horse, I saw another familiar face, though it was no longer an angry face of a horse badly broken. It was now the face of an angel who looked at me as if to say, "What took you so long?" It was the face of the horse I had come to know across the street from Costco, the face of the horse in the *Gringo Gazette* article, and the face of the horse I had branded into my mind as I prayed for all of them each and every night during the longest summer. He turned his face away from his feeder and looked right into my soul. He spoke to me in a language that I understood, and for the first time in a very long time, I knew I was home.

Elizabeth and I got him out of his stall, and then Milagro was groomed and saddled by Saul the caretaker. I wanted so much to do that part, but it seemed Saul took great pride in his establishment, and as a guest, I was to be treated accordingly. Milagro did not have any tack whatsoever of his own, but Saul gathered up enough spare parts for a hackamore bridle. He then saddled Milagro with his personal western saddle, which was very kind of him. He had other horses that he would need to ride, and the cool air of the morning was the perfect time, but he knew this was a big deal for Milagro. Saul had been there to feed and care for him from the very beginning, when he was so weak. Now here he was, ready to join the others out on the trails with a new friend. I could see Saul's twinkle of approval in his eye.

Elizabeth and I talked some more, and she seemed to be sizing me up—not so much what I was saying, but more my physical size. Milagro was a small Baja horse, and she seemed to be pleased that I, too, was on the smaller side. She said, "You are like an Ethiopian. You're perfect for Milagro." I didn't know what sort of comment it was, but I took it as another sign the two of us had found our perfect match.

Together I went with Linda and Fran on what was a routine outing for the two of them. But for me, the transformation was almost instantaneous. With each step on the trail, I felt ever more light and happy. Milagro seemed equally pleased with this invitation to join the others on this beautiful morning. Being the smallest of the three horses, he pressed forward to keep up the pace with his head held high. *A long stride for such a small horse*, I thought to myself. He was not the lagging-behind horse who needed to be prodded along. No, I felt his spirit as a horse with a strong and secure sense of himself, a large ego in a small body, and it just tickled me to no end.

It took an hour or more to make a loop that took us out and around through the desert. October is gorgeous in Cabo. The rains have all cleared, and the humidity from the summer lifts, leaving behind an array of green and flowering trees and shrubs that are magnificent. It's a small window of time, as things turn back to brown by December, so it all just seemed surreal. I thought about the fact that I was in the blooming desert while inside I felt my own soul blossoming open as well.

We returned to the barn sweaty and dusty and happy. Saul took the horses and tied them up for their baths. I handed out carrots while we chatted some more. I thanked Linda and Fran, and without hesitation, they said I was certainly welcome back. And I knew I would be back. Once I opened the door to my heart, there was no closing it. I gathered my things and waved goodbye to Milagro. And I thanked him. With all my heart, I thanked that horse for what he had given me—and for what we were going to become.

That day was magical. I knew it from the moment I woke up in the morning that things were about to change for me. I had no idea to what degree this meeting with Milagro would turn things around for me, but

I was aware that October 11 would now become a day to remember. That day was a turning point for me in ways I cannot explain. All the worry and fear of my upcoming doctor visit and feelings of unrest from living in a foreign land slowly faded away. One by one, they were replaced. The walls were coming down, and in the glory of our first ride together, I could not wipe the smile from my face.

Keith was at the office, so I stopped by on my way home. He was working at his desk in his quiet office upstairs, and as I walked in, he turned to see his dirty, sweaty, happy wife. I could not stop talking about it all, and he sat and listened and smiled. He had lived in the Baja long enough to know it could be a hard and difficult place at times, but at other times, it could bring amazing surprises. He was thrilled for me and genuinely supportive. I explained that Elizabeth would like to lease Milagro to us. That meant we wouldn't take full ownership; we'd just pay for his expenses. And in return, I'd be allowed many more dirty, sweaty, and happy days. It wasn't cheap, as three thousand pesos a month was close to three hundred US dollars. But to my surprise, Keith was totally on board. In his mind, the horse was cheaper than the shrink, and I seemed to get more out of it. And besides, Milagro needed someone too. It was a win all across the board. I sent Elizabeth a text message to say we agreed, and she was thrilled.

And so it was, on an ordinary day like so many before it. I now was the mom to one very special horse. I was needed, and I had a place to go that was sacred and special and all my own, a place that would build me up and chase away the fear as it had done for me so many times in my past—to grow and explore once again on the back of a horse. But this horse was different. I felt a sense of destiny with Milagro that I hadn't felt in a very long time. It was deep. I had been searching for ways to fill that need in me, but I didn't know where to look. I didn't know what I was missing or how to fill the missing part of me. And it wasn't as though I could simply find Milagro. He found me. He chose me. It was as if an invisible string had tied us together and, suddenly, there he was. We needed one another in ways that could not be explained. There was a higher power at work here.

Horse Therapy

THE NEXT WEEK, I had another Skype session scheduled with Lana. I was so excited to tell her about Milagro. I couldn't believe the change I felt in myself in a matter of just a few days. When we logged on, it was good to see her face. I immediately went into the events of the past several days and told her all about Milagro. She listened and smiled and nodded her head in approval, almost as if she wasn't totally surprised by this news. I wondered how often she had the opportunity to witness such a turnaround and how it must have felt for her. There was definitely something bigger than both of us at work here too. We both knew that. What that was didn't need to be discussed. We probably held different views on the matter, but miracles do happen. And for me, this was a turning point in time.

After talking about the exercises and such, she said to me, "Well it seems like you're onto a new path here. Why don't we leave things here for now, and if you need me, you know where to find me." Even my therapist realized that Milagro was now there to carry me along and that her services were no longer necessary.

Getting to Know Milagro

TIME SEEMED TO BE PASSING rather quickly now, and with my new role, I fell into a new routine. After ordering some basic tack necessities for Milagro, we felt as though we had a steady foundation to grow from. He seemed thrilled with having a human of his own, and with each visit came a large, deep whinny upon my arrival. Saul was kind enough to let us use his saddle until I could find one of my own.

My birthday was coming up, and I told Keith that I would like nothing more than to get a saddle for Milagro. He wasn't my horse, so to speak, but we needed one nonetheless. Spending a lot of money on something for a temporary situation was not a good idea, so I set out to find something used.

There was a tack shop in town that was also a

veterinary clinic and feed store all in one. Keith and I took a ride out there, and to my disappointment, the pickings were slim. There were only a few to pick from, and all of them were for the Mexican cowboys—large and heavy with big seats. It seemed that finding something for us was going to be a bit of a challenge.

Fran suggested that I check eBay. So I did, and within a few weeks, I found a reasonably priced all-around western saddle, gently worn and not too heavy. It needed to be a western saddle, as I had never ridden English and wasn't about to start now. Besides, this was what Milagro had always been ridden in while doing his job on the beach. I did my best to measure for fit. We ordered the saddle and waited for it to arrive. Once it made the long journey down through the border, cleared the importation route, and was trucked down the thousand miles, it would be here to stay.

It arrived about a week before my birthday. Since all the deliveries were made to Keith's bodega, he had the guys bring it upstairs and place it near my desk. In large red writing, he wrote "Happy Birthday!" on the box. When I walked in, I was so excited. Finally our saddle was here.

I soon added a lime-green, shiny new halter and lead rope, and a matching rainbow brush and hoof pick as well. To me, this represented the "Somewhere over the Rainbow" song, and he was my pot of gold. Milagro got a few laughs from the ladies, as they thought the rainbows were a bit too feminine for this scrappy horse, but he paid no mind and wore his rainbows with pride. There was a new fly mask, grooming sponges, and giant bottles of fly spray. I wormed him and bought him horse cookies and carrots. And on our visit to the States in December,

I would go to the best tack store in Salt Lake to buy him a specially made saddle pad to help that saddle fit even better. I wanted nothing but the best for my boy, and in true Milagro fashion, he rose to the occasion.

I spent the first weeks at the barn getting to know everyone better. Saul and his wife, their three children, and the other horses. Fran, Linda, and Elizabeth, and their three horses. And of course Milagro. I felt I had known him for eternity, really, like old friends who were reunited. I'd had him branded into my mind all that time during the longest summer. Although I had thought they were rescued, I still never forgot his face: the fiery red gelding with the white fishhook blaze. His spirit never left me. And now here we were, together as friends, as family. Just the very thought of Milagro now brought a smile to my face. I walked proudly and carried myself with a newfound confidence. His very being lifted me.

Learning about what had actually happened during the longest summer was utterly heartbreaking, though. After the disappearance of the horses in the fall of the longest summer, the man who owned them did respond to the public shaming from the *Gringo Gazette* article—but not in the way the public had hoped. He decided he was getting too much attention with them being out there for everyone to see, so he rounded them up and hid them from sight. When many others like me thought that something had been done to save them, we were dead wrong—they continued in that desperate situation for months. From September all the way through to the first of December, he continued to deprive them of the necessities, of the things that anyone with half a heart knew they needed—food, water, care. So while we all drove the four-lane passing the Costco, bidding a sigh of relief, there had been no relief whatsoever. The painful suffering had continued.

This was when Elizabeth had stepped in. She knew this man, and she had been around long enough to know how to get something done. She had gone and taken the worst of them. And with the help of the president of the Humane Society at the time, who happened to be bilingual, she was able to get proper documentation and notarized documents to protect Milagro. The papers were vital so that this man could not show up on her doorstep months later, wanting his now-healthy horse back, which had been known to happen. She took Milagro when he was at his worst and brought him to Saul's barn, where there just so happened to be one stall open. This was where the real rescue had happened. And even though she and I had crossed paths right after this, I never knew it was Milagro. I never knew it was the red gelding with the fishhook blaze. Because in my mind, and in so many others', they had been saved long ago.

Milagro came to Saul's barn, and with food, water, and love, he flourished. There were no lifesaving IVs of fluids or miracle veterinary care. He was given a place to heal. And in time, he began to do so. He was eventually turned out for exercise just like the others. Although his legs swelled in the beginning, and it was hard, he never gave in. And in time, he grew ever so strong. He made friends with the horses, and he was treated with respect and dignity. No one really knew if he would make it. But after ten months of this, he grew strong enough that it was time for him to start riding again. And that's when I met Milagro.

He seemed to say, "You can see these lines across my face, telling a story of where I've been, telling a story of my life and of the troubles that I have faced, but these lines are not there to bring sorrow. Don't let these lines define me, as if you promise to keep digging, you will find my spirit, and that is where the truth lies. That is where you will find the real me. The real Milagro."

I don't see the scars anymore. It took me some time to get past the roadmap of abuse on Milagro's body, from the top of his head, where the big white scars sat from a poorly fitting bridle, to the even larger white patches that lined his belly and girth from the painful saddles cinched on top of open wounds—hard leather meeting his skeletal-thin body lined with painful wounds. Once the work began, these wounds would fill with dripping sweat. The leather and girth would rub back and forth, day after day, against his delicate body until eventually the hair fell out and open wounds lay in its place. When the hair finally came back, it grew in white, as if an angel had kissed them to make them heal.

There were the damaged muscles that protruded from his neck and chest, hard balls of muscle that, after one traumatic event or another, gave in and snapped. They pulled away and balled up in a sign of surrender, likely muscle tears from extended labor with little rest. How it must have felt to be pushed to continue the work. Surrender was never an option for Milagro. His spirit wouldn't allow it.

There were the missing patches of fur from the rain rot that had set in on his back and his legs, itching open sores caused by uncleanliness and bacteria that eventually rotted his skin to the point it died in places. The hair there would never grow back—a sacrifice given against his will.

Each day, he would carry tourists up and down the beach. Those who paid a dollar more were allowed the thrill of running him along the beach. In heavy sand and blistering heat and humidity, up and down the beach they went. Had they no idea what this animal endured?

Every day, Milagro and his herd would be rounded up, cinched up, and tied up to stand all day in the beating sun only to be subjected to the clueless antics of unknowing tourists who had nothing better to do with their time. But in their defense, they would not have known. The visible wounds and scars of the horses were carefully covered with saddles and bridles so as not to call attention. It wasn't as though the horses could speak for themselves. This was their reality. Going out each day to turn tricks like a hooker for their john, Milagro and his amigos had to put on a happy face for a happy ending. And with that, they earned their food and water.

On the bottom of his front legs were rings of white fur, possibly from wearing hobbles or getting caught up in barbed wire while trying to find food out in the vast open desert. He had squirrely lines that could only be seen in the middle of summer, when his coat was thin and flat. The desert is full of cactus with spines and sharp prickles. And when a horse is hungry enough, he will endure the pain to push through such things for his survival—pushing through nature's barbed walls and man's barbed wire all for a bite of food.

The white patches that covered his hip bones were some of the hardest for me to get over. Unlike the other scars that were made when he could still muster strength and dignity, these white patches were from the time when he came so close to death. These were scars from when he was too weak to move, too weak to fight, and he simply laid his tired body down on the earth in abandonment, when he must have felt so utterly alone and defeated, when the only thing that had kept him going was his will to survive, when he was wrestled to the ground like a demon and all that was left to do was lie down and give in, his thin, frail bones protruding against the hard ground until the skin broke and gaping sores crept in. These were the scars that not only angered me but also frightened me. Because they told me just how close he was to crossing to the dark side.

Yet still, under all the ugliness of his life, after all

these lines and scars and sorrow, his spirit soared. It stretched beyond imagination and reached into my heart as if to say "No, that is not who I am. I am much, much more than any story of scars and sadness. I am Milagro, and I have the spirit of a great warrior. My ancestors sailed the ocean blue with great conquerors." His pride and his spirit were never broken. *He* was never broken.

Riding

IN THE FALL, the desert is an inviting place. The rolling hills that stand brown and empty most of the year suddenly turn thick, lush, and green. Vines begin to bloom and creep. Hard, twisting trees grow soft leaves and change shape. The pointy stark lines of each plant diminish, and there is no beginning or end. They all become one, all vying for Mother Nature's blessing of pollination to ensure the future propagation. It's as if they wake up and decide to shake hands with their neighbors. Then they dance in unison, arms linked as they look up to the sky and smile.

Riding Milagro through this desert for the first time was simply magic. It was a small loop around a piece of property that had been sheltered from development. Just a short distance from homes and hotels, we found this perfect paradise. The quietness and tranquility was breathtaking. The sound of his hooves meeting the ground and the squeak of the leather beneath me all intertwined with the birds chirping. It was magnificent. I'd lived around this terrain for two years now but only experienced it while passing by in a car. There were miles and miles of desert that seemed to have no end. I never gave much thought to what the details might be. To me, it was just a vast open space left wild and untamed. But here we were, Milagro and me, climbing hills, winding down old dirt roads that were left from another time. He knew this desert well and made me feel welcome, as if he, too, held out his hand to welcome me.

It was an amazing place I had been invited to share, one that most tourists or even full-time residents rarely get a chance to experience. It was by invitation only, and I had made the short list. With Milagro as my royal steed, we entered the chambers of the glorious, rigorous, and untamed Baja Desert. Surrounded by all of the beauty and life that was popping up around us, it felt like a new beginning. It was as if the desert was there to give its blessing to this new union of one of its children and his new friend. I never felt more grateful in all my life. Our rides were simple yet spectacular each time. We went out with or without our barn friends. Either way, it brought us closer. I had a new role as Milagro's chosen one, and I took great pride in this role. And I had a renewed strength for what lay ahead.

Meeting Dr. Peters

IT WAS KEITH'S BIRTHDAY, and we were packed and on our way to the airport. Flying to Salt Lake City for my long-awaited doctor appointment meant we could combine it to enjoy some winter weather. Skiing was Keith's favorite activity, and he had been working so hard. I felt so happy for him to be able to get some time off, and for us to enjoy the mountains we loved, together. We would be spending Christmas there as well. We both shared an adoration for the Christmas season. And with Milagro's recent effect of wearing down my fear and anxiety, and replacing it with hope, the fact that it was Christmastime had the same effect as well. It was almost impossible for me to feel down. I had too much to be thankful for.

A few days after we arrived, it was time for our meeting with Dr. Peters. We drove to the University of Utah Neurosciences Center, parked, and went inside. I filled out the many forms that were required, provided them with my insurance card, and paid the copay, and then we waited patiently for them to call my name.

It wasn't long before we were in a room, and soon came a knock on the door. Dr. Peters walked in, shook my hand, and introduced himself as well as his fellow. The first thing I noticed was his tie. It had Golden Retrievers all over it. I instantly felt at ease.

Dr. Peters not only was an expert in the field of MS and neurology but also had dedicated his life to the study and treatment of patients with MS. As a long-standing member of the staff, he had earned a very distinguished reputation. I was happy to be able to see someone with such experience. His genuine care and concern came as a wonderful surprise. He was not rushed, and he listened very patiently to whatever I was telling him. After our questions and answers, and then the physical exam, he didn't say anything that was alarming. I waited for the big ball to drop. The big announcement that would change my life forever never came. Instead, he listened and nodded along to what I was telling him, as if he understood. And he never sounded any alarm.

Dr. Peters never told me that I had MS that day. He never told me I was to do this or that, or to expect this or that. Instead, he helped me start to open my mind to the gray area that surrounds a disease like MS. It didn't mean I didn't have it, and he wanted to see me in another three months, and then another. He didn't release me and say it didn't exist, but he also didn't send me down a rabbit hole. He knew that in this gray area, where there was not enough to warrant medications and a loaded line of attack, there was also no need to get me all worked up. To worry would only cause harm. We needed to harness a more disciplined approach, a wait-and-watch approach.

It's hard to describe how this approach felt at first. As someone who had waited six months, worrying about whether or not I was going to become a cripple, I wanted answers. But I didn't want the wrong answers. And if the approach was a wait-and-see sort of "no news is good news" approach, I had to learn to be OK with that. On one hand, his not telling me the big bad announcement was wonderful news. But not getting a solid answer was a bit hard to accept at first. I think if it hadn't been for Milagro softening me and bringing me back around to living for the moment, I might not have handled this approach very well at all. But life isn't always full of answers. What I was thankful for at the end of our first of many visits was that I had a caring, compassionate, patient doctor who wore a tie with Golden Retrievers on it. I felt very fortunate.

Keith and I celebrated this news with many days of skiing and time spent fireside, drinking warm holiday drinks. The snow continued to fall like it always does. The sun rose and fell. It was the best trip, and one of so much relief. Each day after my meeting with Dr. Peters, I let that horrible anticipation fall by the wayside. The layers of fear that Milagro had helped to chip away at melted and stayed behind on that trip. I came home a new and grateful person. I knew I wasn't in the clear, by any means, but I had the right sources of support now. I had Keith, Roy, and now Milagro and Dr. Peters. I had a feeling it would be a very good year.

Healing Together

IN A BIZARRE WAY, Milagro built a bridge between the Cabo I was experiencing and the one I was meant to know. I slowly began to grow outside the bubble I found comfortable and began to own this new life here in Cabo rather than shy away from it. I found myself embracing this special place. Like Roy, who needed to get out for walks each day, Milagro had certain needs that took me outside my comfort zone.

Besides the feed Saul secured for the barn, rabbit pellets were the only form of extra protein we could find for the horses. So I took my turn in rotation with Elizabeth in providing these for Milagro and her horse, Carlos. The only place that sold *conejina* was the little feed store back deep in the *barrio*. I had a territory where I drove in Cabo, and the feed store was outside my safety zone. But soon I was out there following directions like "look for the church" and "then turn right at the tire store," going around and around the *barrio* until I found it, a small red building with a black-and-white checkered wall that symbolized the sale of Purina products.

In front of the converted old house was what would have been the front yard but had now been turned into pens for small animals and chickens. Inside, I found freshly swept dirt floors, a ceiling fan, and banda music playing. There were two men working, and it was a busy place, mostly with chicken farmers, or perhaps chicken fighters. They sold a small variety of vet supplies, like flea and tick control for dogs and special medications for farm animals. The only things that were specific to horses were fly spray and a product called Red Cell that made the racehorses go faster. Those horses, like Milagro, had been born to work too. Yet they had a different job to do, and the stakes were much higher. His job of riding people up and down the beach was one thing. These horses only got a few shots to prove themselves worthy. They were born with the necessity to run and win. Each and every time, they needed to win. And when they didn't win, there was never room for second best.

I stood in line and waited. As soon as they asked what I needed, I swiftly and proudly announced that I needed a large bag of conejina. I had learned that speaking in Spanish fast and in an affirming way was how the Mexican women spoke—no need to smile or dally along. As much as this was truly a novelty to me, I needed to get down to business. Feed stores had always been a place of fascination for me, but this was no time to explore. I had a mission and needed to convey my position as one of confidence—never mind my lululemon gym clothes, brightly colored Salomon tennis shoes, Tory Burch handbag, and SUV with Utah plates. This was such a stretch for me, and I was always so nervous. Luckily, with the rotation, I only had to make it out there every couple months. But it was never a question. I was a horse mom, and in these parts, this was what we horse moms needed to do.

In the spring, we took another trip up to Salt Lake to see Dr. Peters. This meeting was very similar to the first, and after talking and sharing information back and forth, he did a physical exam. All seemed to be about the same as before, which was very good news to hear. He asked to see me again in June, so we set out on this routine of seeing each other every three months.

We returned home and enjoyed what was left of the lovely spring season. My days felt more fulfilling now, as I had not only Roy and Keith to care for but Milagro as well. Our friendships with the ladies at the barn grew. My Spanish improved while I tried my best to communicate with Saul and his family. Things were running on autopilot, and I was feeling very blessed.

The summer was coming, and I knew what the heat did to my energy, and my body in general. I was worried about how I would get out and ride as often with the summer creeping in. We'd had a lovely several months of cooler temps together. The glorious beauty of fall led to winter and then spring. Our rides out through the desert had been so amazing, and Milagro and I bonded even further. He whinnied at me when I got to the barn to see him. Some days, I just went out and brushed him, gave him carrots, and let him into the back pasture to graze. I'd bring a book, sit and read, and watch him saunter about. Just spending time with him put a smile on my face. And our special barn with our little family was such a warm and welcome place.

Some days, we rode in the arena, which was nicely built and large with good sand footing and white rails. It sat raised above the lower acreage next door, with a view of the Arch and the Medano Bay. Some days, there would be cruise ships in port. We would trot around and stop under the shade of the palm tree and take in the view. It was such a beautiful time for us, growing together and learning about each other.

But summer was creeping in. The temperatures were rising, and I had to find something to help me get through the coming months. I did some research and found a cooling vest with panels of frozen chambers that went on the front and back. The vest fit tightly and, over a cotton long-sleeved shirt, created just enough of a buffer from the toxic heat of the summer to get us out and about. Mornings were the only reasonable chance at getting in a ride. We always fought the clock to get there as early as possible to capture what was left of the cool of the night. But nothing was going to keep me from Milagro. So with a cooling vest and a cooling bandana, I would set out and get our rides in.

The other ladies had years of acclimating that I didn't have. But the issues my body presented were also a unique challenge. The high I got from riding always offset the lows from the extreme temperatures, and Milagro guided me. He made it all too easy. He never put up a fuss and always made our outings such fun. He needed it as much as I did. This poor horse had spent years with a poor broken body, and now he was healthy and renewed. We both enjoyed this new lease on life.

Roy's Trip

AROUND THE TIME I was starting to really feel settled, I began to notice a large lump in Roy's neck. It was on top of his windpipe, and it was hard and large. It had been there for some time but recently seemed larger, and his breathing was a bit more labored. I had my appointment set with Dr. Peters in late August, and after Keith and I discussed it further, we decided that I should take Roy along with me. There were veterinarians in Cabo, but unfortunately the education and laboratory advancements in the States had not made it down south. Routine care like shots and such were fine, but for this type of thing, I wanted to have the best and most accurate information possible. I changed my flight so that we could stay for a week, and I rented a pet-friendly condo where he could stay. I hoped that we would get good news at both our appointments and return to our happy life.

Some people have pets; others have fur children—that's how it was with Roy and me. He was the second of two very special Labradors in my life. And as the second baby, and the one I had more time to bond with, he was by far the best fur friend I had ever had. Together, we had been through so much. Roy had been there to get me through the roughest of times. And it wasn't just that; I loved Roy like a child, like family. He was my baby, and I was a mother bear who would go to the ends of the earth to fight for and protect him. It was the closest I'd ever felt to being a mother, and really, he was my boy. So when I felt this lump and talked to our vet in Park City, and she encouraged me to bring him up for an evaluation, I knew it had to be done. The fears I had about my own health truly took a back seat to my worry for him.

We flew up on a Monday, and by the end of the day, we were checked into our condo. I had rented a minivan with sliding side doors so that he could get in easily. Roy's comfort came first.

Roy seemed giddy about being back in Park City. The smell of the grass and critters and crisp mountain air had him smiling and bouncing about.

His appointment was the following morning. I had been in conversation with Dr. Bernard since I first felt this lump, so she was aware of how things had progressed. And after only a few minutes, as if she figured I already knew, she told me she thought it was most likely a tumor. I asked her, "A cancer tumor?" "Yes," she said, "a thyroid tumor."

We talked some more, and tears began to slide down my cheeks. The dreaded life-changing sentence I had anticipated with Dr. Peters but never heard was suddenly ringing in my ears as we sat and talked about my Roy. I was completely caught off guard and had not prepared myself for this. We talked about what tests she wanted to do to confirm her opinion, and also to possibly stage the cancer. Stage the cancer? I thought. Wait, this was moving way too fast. But we quickly made the appointment to do the guided needle aspiration and ultrasound the following day. She walked us to the door, and Roy bolted through it. He hadn't heard one word or mention of cancer. All he knew was that he had been sprung free from the hospital, and now this meant a ride in the car and some goodies. As I loaded him into the minivan and turned to drive away, I caught a glimpse of him in the rearview mirror. Mouth wide open, tongue hanging out, and nose held high to the fresh air outside the window. How would I ever break the news to him?

We went to the McDonald's drive-through on the way home. I had skipped breakfast, and Roy was always up for a warm bun filled with eggs, cheese, and bacon. I let him sniff the warm paper bag, and I drove the half mile to the condo. His drool was hanging to the floor by the time we arrived, so I let him eat his outside the car. Two seconds later, it was gone—not a single sign of that Egg McMuffin.

After I had a chance to eat my breakfast, and share with Roy of course, I called Keith. I had composed myself to take this news in short successions. Today would be about accepting the possibility of cancer. Keith and I talked, and he shared his disappointment with me. We knew tomorrow's test would be the final word, so we let it end at that. He said, "We don't know anything for certain, so let's just hope for the best."

I dropped Roy off at the vet at eight o'clock the following morning. He had never in his life been left at the vet except for when he was neutered as a young pup. It would only be a few hours, but it was heartbreaking for me. I set out to do some shopping for things we could use back in Cabo to make the time go faster. I kept busy prepping our condo for our guest, as my friend Donna would be arriving from San Diego that same day. I was so happy she was coming. It had been a nice idea to share a few days together while she took some time away from work and the kids. Now I felt guilty that I was a wreck worrying about Roy. But once she arrived, it would all work out. That's what friends are for.

The phone rang shortly after noon. It was time to pick up Roy. I raced over to the vet, and he was eager to be sprung from doggie jail once again. They told me that Dr. Bernard would review the tests and call me as soon as she could.

I took him home to the condo. He seemed excited, but I knew it was nervous energy and, at the age of ten, he would be tired from the ordeal. After a short walk, I settled him in and then left for the airport to pick up Donna.

It was wonderful to see her, and such a nice distraction at the same time. Donna and I had been friends for thirty years. Her cheerful personality and upbeat spirit gave Roy and me both the shot in the arm that we needed. It would be the following day before I got the results, so we put that aside for the time being and set out to have some fun. We took Roy on his favorite walk up near the McPolin Farm and their famous white barn. He started to yowl and talk in the car as we got close, as he remembered his favorite spot! We spent time resting and relaxing with a couple glasses of wine by the fireplace in the condo, talking and talking. It never ceases to amaze me how much we girls can talk. But it was so wonderful, and by the end of that night, we were all relaxed and had a very good night's sleep.

The following day was open, and Donna and I had planned on hiking. I was anxious to hear about Roy, so I called and left a message for Dr. Bernard. She called me back not long after and apologized, saying she'd had an emergency surgery. Then she went on to tell me that, yes, her instincts were correct and it was a tumor. We could not stage the tumor, though, because thyroid tumors are very vascular and it is not safe to do a biopsy, which also meant it was not safe to do surgery to remove the tumor. Doing radiation or chemotherapy had not been shown to help these types of tumors either. So we could only hope it was a slow-growing tumor, and with the way it had been on his neck for some time, we could only hope it would continue to be slow growing.

That was it. There was nothing we could do, not anything that was humane or ethical for a dog of ten years and with the location of the tumor. No chemo, or radiation. He had this and we could only hope for the best.

I called and let Keith know the results. He knew I was torn up about it, and there were no right words to say, just that Roy was happy and in good spirits and that the vet had no recommendations to change that. We had nothing to offer him either, except a wait-and-see approach. I was getting a bit tired of this wait-and-see approach. But what else could we do? We had to just accept it, appreciate him each and every day, and hope he would continue in a positive manner.

Donna and I enjoyed our few days together. It was really special to see her and have that support. After she left, I had my appointment with Dr. Peters, and I had my fingers crossed that I would get a good checkup. After the recent news about Roy, I really couldn't take any more bad news. And just as it had been at my previous appointments, all seemed to be going well and I was holding steady and having no further decline. I scheduled my next appointment to see him in six months. Then Roy and I set out to make our way back to Cabo.

Hurricane Odile

KEITH AND I HAD A FEW WEEKS before our pre-planned trip to visit family in San Diego and take a vacation to Chicago. It was September now, and hurricane season had been off to a lively start. Cabo had been spared by a few named storms already. The alphabet was ticking its way down, and the most recent storm, Norbert, spun close enough to bring rain and wind but nothing we all couldn't handle.

I felt terrible about leaving Roy after learning of his cancer, but I knew he would be in the best of hands. Our friends and pet sitter would be staying at the house. They were in the loop on Roy's health, and we left them with a lot of handwritten notes and special vitamins and supplements I had gotten for him. I hugged him hard as we left for the airport. It was a nine-day trip. We would be home soon.

We got to San Diego and settled into my brother's house. We were all enjoying the weekend together. But Keith and I were keeping a close eye on things back home. A small named storm that had formed days earlier was now growing in strength. By the time Saturday rolled around, this hurricane was becoming a dangerous threat. It seemed that this one would make landfall. With Mother Nature, no one knows for sure. But this storm seemed to be tracking itself directly towards Cabo.

By Sunday afternoon, it was imminent. Hurricane Odile, now a Category 4 storm, was headed straight for Cabo and would make a direct hit. A picture from NASA showed the hugest, scariest thing I'd ever seen. The size of the hurricane compared to the little tip of Baja just astounded me. I spoke with our pet sitter once more and offered her the tips for this and that inside our home. I felt so bad that we were not there for our animals, for our home and the business, and for Milagro. This was a monster storm, and we were helpless up in the States.

I went to bed that night knowing that as we all lay down in a quiet and safe home, our friends, our family, were bracing as the hurricane was rolling in. A few posts on Facebook were already surfacing. One friend posted that she was locked in the bathroom with water running through her house and that a large transformer for power had blown up. I just couldn't fathom that this was happening. I watched for more Facebook posts. And then nothing, the newsfeed went silent.

It was Monday morning, and Keith and I were scheduled to leave on our flight for Chicago. My brother turned on the morning news, and immediately we saw coverage from the devastation in Cabo. Standing in the living room so far from our home, I watched the footage and saw the destruction. Places I knew were just utterly destroyed. Cars and power lines blown about like leaves in the wind. The hotels on the beach hit so hard that swimming pools were falling into the ocean. It made national news, and that alone meant it was bad, really bad.

We wanted to go home instead of flying to Chicago, but we couldn't. The Cabo airport had been completely destroyed and torn apart. The newly constructed airport had the roof torn off, and inside it looked as though a bomb had exploded. The walls were in shreds. And the fact that we could not fly there meant that none of the tourists could fly out.

I messaged our pet sitter through Facebook Messenger. Phones were down. No text messages or phone calls were going through. Somehow, though, through the messenger app on Facebook, we were able to communicate. She and her husband were OK. They had all made it safely through the night, and luckily our house hadn't lost any windows, which kept it mostly intact. There had been some flooding, but we had done well. Roy and Kitty were safe and had been sequestered to the laundry room during the storm. They all rode out the night of terror, and as the sun rose the next morning, the damage was evident.

I tried my best to get information about Milagro. It took three days before I could get a message through, and

Fran was finally able to reply that they all were safe. The barn had lost some structures and there was damage, but the stalls were intact and Saul and his family were safe. The water had rushed right past the stalls, into the lower part of the property, and pushed down walls in that area. Fortunately Saul was on-site and could bucket up enough water from the cistern for the horses, and there was enough hay that had been protected. But the horses were sequestered to their stalls for the time being.

Fran, though, could not even drive the distance from her house to the barn due to the roads being flooded and full of debris and power lines. But at least I finally heard how they were all doing. The waiting had been excruciating. I had worried that it might have been necessary to turn the horses out to run for safety. I had heard before that depending on how storms came in, it could become necessary to turn them out so as not to lose them to flooding in their stalls. This thought had kept me awake at night, wondering where Milagro was and what was happening. To hear from Fran that the stalls were fine and the horses were doing well was such a tremendous relief.

We spent a week in Chicago and then flew back to San Diego instead of going home, as the Cabo airport was still closed. After waiting another week in San Diego, Keith was able to get a flight into La Paz. His engineer got word that the road was passable, so he drove the two hours up to get Keith and bring him back to Cabo. Up until this point, it was impossible to get down there. And resources were slim, so no one wanted to pull from the scarce supplies that existed in town. But once Keith got to leave, it was a huge relief for him. He didn't need me in the way and didn't want to worry about my well-being, so we agreed that I would stay behind at my brother's until the airport opened and things were more stable.

Once I dropped Keith off at the airport, I suddenly had second thoughts about staying behind. How much I had wanted to go home, to see my friends and be back with Roy and Milagro. I wanted to help. I hated feeling so helpless and so far away from my home, my family. But this was not the time to think about myself. Keith needed to stay laser focused to be able to help his people back home. And I knew that his being there to take over would be a great relief.

I continued to wait it out in San Diego. This hurricane had been like no other. And it was the largest documented hurricane to hit the Baja in history. No one knew how to deal with this kind of damage. I was helpless, and each day, I waited for the news that it was time to go home.

I received a message from a friend that Alaska Airlines had just opened up one flight into Cabo. It had been about four weeks now with not one single commercial flight going into Cabo. This one flight was from LAX, and I had to get a seat. So I quickly called, and with their caring customer support, I secured one for myself. My friends from Seattle had been in the same situation and were waiting to return home. I would meet them there, and together we would make our way back home.

The day could not come soon enough. I drove up and booked a room at the airport the day before the flight just to make sure I would be there on time. I didn't want to take any chances with trying to drive from San Diego to Los Angeles early in the morning. So once I returned the rental car I had been driving for those three weeks, I checked into my hotel and waited.

The following morning, I took the shuttle to the airport, and when I checked in for my flight, I found out that Alaska Airlines had created a special desk specifically for the flight to Cabo. They knew there was special attention needed that day and a lot of people would have a lot of questions. I didn't have any questions. I just wanted to get through these next few hours and finally be home.

I saw my friends, and we hugged with tears in our eyes. We could not contain the emotion we all felt. Being kept from our homes, our pets, and our lives—it hurt. With all the excitement about going home, we also were able to finally let down our guard and begin to feel what had been kept inside during those past weeks. The worry and the concern had carved out space in our hearts, and even though we didn't know exactly what we were going home to, that space was beginning to fill back in with a level of comfort and closure.

This flight was like no other I'd ever been on or any I will likely fly again. Not one person was napping or reading. We were a mixed bag of passengers, many of whom had evacuated shortly after the storm and also those of us who had been stranded in the US, waiting to go home. There were two brides onboard whose weddings were to take place, so they were making their way down to fulfill their dreams. We all talked, and there were many *cervezas* being served to try to dampen our anxiety. We were all bonded in a special way that day.

It was such a surreal feeling when we landed that afternoon. It struck me to look out over the tarmac and realize that not one single plane had landed there bringing tourists or residents for so many weeks. The plane seemed to quiet down, and as we taxied to the jetway, everyone let out a big sigh of relief. But also a dose of reality hung in the air, as we all were headed into the unknown. Each passenger had a unique and different purpose that day.

The vibe had turned a bit more serious, but then we noticed something outside the plane. There was a fire engine that had driven up alongside us and was suddenly spraying our plane with water! The stewardess came on the intercom right away to announce that no there wasn't a fire; it was the local fire department welcoming us back to Cabo. What a sight that was, and everyone quickly changed their attitude, and smiles were on all our faces.

And the celebration continued. As we walked from the plane, down the skyway, we could hear mariachis playing. The music echoed off the large marble floors, and the sound was beautiful. Vendors from all different areas of tourism were there, shaking our hands, handing out cold beer and water, smiling, welcoming us all back. My emotions could not be contained. These people had been through it all. And here they were, giving us a huge welcome. The level of gratitude I felt was astonishing.

Keith had parked and was waiting inside for me. We hugged and held each other. I told him all about the big welcome we had received. Finally, we were back on Cabo soil, together. I was never so happy and felt I'd never want to leave this place ever again.

There was only one thing to do that afternoon. After seeing Roy and Kitty and our home, I unpacked a bit, and then we just had to go to the beach. So we put on our suits and headed to one of our favorite places.

What a sight—it was as though Cabo had entered a time machine and gone back twenty years or more. There were very few people on the beach. The restaurant we went to had just a few tables set out. No music, no vendors, no jet skis or cruise ships. There weren't any boats in the bay. There were small waves lapping up onto the sand. We could look up and down Medano Beach and see only a handful of people. The place was quiet and still. It was as beautiful as I'd ever seen it. We had some drinks and ceviche, and watched the sky turn into pale shades of pink and blue before the sun set for good that day. Life would return to normal the next morning, and my next stop would be the barn, to see Milagro. Finally.

Beyond the Fences

IT WAS SO GOOD to finally get home and feel settled after being displaced for so long. I felt that I had taken this place for granted. I was so excited to see Milagro. I planned to meet at the barn and ride with Linda and her horse, Chief. I bundled up a bag of carrots and water bottles. Outfitted with my trusty cooling vest, which had proven to be a good investment, I headed to the barn.

Linda and I set out that morning with no real direction in mind. Once we got going, she said in her playful manner, "Hey, why don't we go ride across the road, on the beach!" All the fences that had kept us from doing so in the past had blown down during the hurricane. It would be weeks before the wood and barbed wire were replaced. We thought this was too good an opportunity to miss.

Her idea proved to be correct. The fields of land across the street from our barn were now wide-open spaces. Any debris that would have been there had long been swept out to sea, as had all the fences. We trotted along packed dirt roads until we reached the sand and grassy dunes that lined the historic Medano Beach. The horses seemed excited by the change of scenery. Milagro pushed forward with strength and curiosity. He kept pace with Chief, who was much larger than Milagro, sometimes even taking the lead. I wondered if he had worked these beaches before, in his career. Maybe they had been hard to handle when he was in that weakened state. But now that he had recovered and his body felt better, I thought he might just be showing off a bit. *Bravo*, which means "brave." He seemed to enjoy every bit of this ride.

We crested the sand dune and stopped to take in the view. Out in front of us was the famous El Arco, the Arch of Los Cabos. The ocean was glistening silver and deep blue as the sunshine reflected off the gentle current of the bay. There was a breeze blowing, and I looked down and watched as the wind took up the ends of Milagro's mane and curled them upwards. His tiny forelock that hung between his ears whistled in the wind.

Linda and I reveled in the beauty. Even though this town had been battered very badly, the essence and charm of Cabo withstood the storm. I could feel the pulse of perseverance that resonated not only from Milagro but also from Cabo itself. This tiny place had a heartbeat all its own, sometimes not in step with mine. But today we were all beating together as one.

Linda loved to say "Let's ride like the wind." And so as we turned to head home, the horses began to gallop. My smile broke into full-fledged laughter as I held on to Milagro. This place was full of surprises. It was full of something special.

Crossroads

AS HORRIBLE AS HURRICANE ODILE HAD BEEN for Cabo, it had been good for business. Keith's employees had worked seven days a week from the middle of September all the way through December. The yearly *posada* had been a welcomed event that signaled the slowing of business and some breathing room for all.

All this business also meant profits had improved. As for Keith and me, we started to think about our five-year plan. We were coming up on four years, and our plan had never been to stay in Cabo. Our time there was to help Keith get the business back on its feet. Our goal had always been to get the business over the trauma of the Great Recession. The plan was never to make Cabo a long-term stay. The years leading up to the hurricane had been strong and steady. And now with this latest shot in the arm, it seemed that rethinking our five-year plan was in order.

Back in San Diego, our parents were facing some medical challenges. My mom continued to decline into the throes of Alzheimer's. Keith's father was facing a double hip replacement, and his mother, who had suffered a stroke, needed constant supervision to keep her from wandering or getting into trouble. We felt guilty that, up to this point, our contributions had been from a distance. This meant that our siblings who lived in San Diego had to be hands-on with all their care. As much as we had wanted to go back to Park City, San Diego was calling. And as we entered the New Year, we began to really think hard about this possibility.

Things had started out pretty roughly for me in Mexico. I had much difficulty adjusting to living abroad. Truthfully, I hadn't really found my place until the year before, when I met Milagro. Once he came into my life, I felt I belonged. I had gained that priceless sense of worth that I had lost. The year leading up to the hurricane had been magical. And the month I was held away from my home because of Hurricane Odile had only strengthened the sense of home and community I had finally come to know. The essence of this beautiful, complicated, and, yes, challenging environment had sunk deep into my heart. What had this meant to me? I had grown to love this place. I had found my sense of purpose, one that had been growing with me my entire life. And along with Keith and Roy, there was Milagro. My miracle. In my wildest of dreams, I would never have imagined getting to this place. I just couldn't gather my thoughts around it.

But this had been the plan all along. I talked to Keith and told him that I was not in a hurry to go. Yes, it was the plan. But I needed him to be certain. The person who, a few years back, would have been packing my bags at the very mention of moving back to the States was now pulling back from that idea. And as I dived deeper into understanding why, I knew it was Milagro. Our things would be packed, and Roy and Kitty would fly with us just as we had done before, but there was no plan for Milagro.

It was a difficult crossroads with my heart telling me one thing but my head another. During all this time I had spent with Milagro, I told myself I would never leave him behind. I had dreams of Milagro back in Park City, amongst the tall green grasses in pastures set beneath mountains topped with snow, on long sunny days that were never too hot for rides. I dreamt of the two of us riding along mountain streams, with the colors of fall around us. I always knew we would leave Cabo. And in my dreams, Milagro would come with us. It was just the way it would be. But here I was, facing the reality that we would be moving, and I had no idea what to do about Milagro.

A Shared Dream

I TOLD KEITH I wanted to bring him with us. He asked me how this was going to happen. And I had no idea. It was a pipe dream, and Keith knew what everyone else knew: Horses like Milagro never left Cabo. He'd driven the road and experienced its thousand-plus miles of twisting and winding roads, the heat across the desert, and the multiple checkpoints. At the end of that road was a border that had rules for bringing anything across to the other side—including a horse like Milagro.

I began to ask the ladies at the barn, and they gave me the same downward smile that told me to lay this dream to rest. I wasn't serious about this plan, was I? He was a Mexican horse, one meant to live out his days there in the quiet seaside town. Even my most animal-loving friends gave me the look, one that said "It's time to lay this dream to rest." There were no words of hope or encouragement, only the unspoken words that tried to break it to me gently. Horses like Milagro weren't meant for such a dream.

Milagro, on the other hand, did share this dream with me. As we rode, I would talk to him and tell him he was going to be taking a very long journey soon. I told him he would need his strength and he needed to trust me. He would have to leave the home he had grown to know. But he was going to a new place where he would be happy. I would be there, and we would do amazing things together. And I would never leave him. He would listen and perk up his ears, and his body would tighten and his head would be held high. I told him that, above all else, he had to believe in me because I needed him on my side. And so together we worked on building strength and looked for guidance as I set out to get this horse to the USA.

Losing Hope

IT WAS THREE WEEKS before our move, and I still had not come up with a plan. Each day, it was as if I expected some brilliant idea to reveal itself. But as each day came and went, I still had no idea how to get Milagro up north. Keith was so busy trying to tie up loose ends that I didn't ask for help from him. I also knew he had nothing to offer. The days of living in denial were coming to an end. Something had to give. And the very reality of having to leave Milagro behind was hitting me squarely in the face. My heart was aching, and I knew that it could not take the heartbreak of leaving him behind. I simply couldn't lose another horse.

Dandy's Departure

MY CHILDHOOD DREAM had been short lived, and the love and friendship I shared with Dandy had been taken from me. Together, Dandy and I had about five good years before the bottom fell out. My mom and Phil did their best to shelter us kids from the truth. But as we got older and wiser, it didn't take much to figure things out.

Phil's drinking had become a silent danger in our house. As anyone who grew up with an alcoholic parent knows, the denial can only hold on for so long. I was older now, and it was hard to have friends over, not knowing who or what kind of dad was going to show his face that day. My mom tried to intervene and, with the doctor's help, got him medication, the kind that would make him sick if he drank. But he learned to substitute it for aspirin, and the fight with the demons inside this good man continued.

I was now a freshman in high school. My older brother had moved away, and my middle brother would often butt heads with our stepdad. Phil was not a violent drinker— until one day, he was. That was the day my mother told him she was leaving him. He held her at gunpoint for a few hours in front of our house while they sat on the tailgate of our flatbed truck. It ended peacefully with the neighbors calling the sheriff to intervene. Phil gave in to the encouragement from the sheriff to put the gun down. And it ended. And that was the beginning of the worst of it for me. As the walls caved in on my family, the world I knew and loved and trusted quickly, and without discussion, came to an end as well.

I denied this truth to myself for some time but eventually willed myself to ask my mother the question that hung in the air like a vice around my neck. What were we going to do with the animals? I knew she and Phil were going their separate ways. I did not know exactly what that meant for me, or for Dandy and all the other animals I loved so much: my goats and sheep I showed in 4-H, the ducks, the rabbits, the dogs, and the cats. But mostly the deeply rooted fear I had was of losing Dandy. So I asked. And with one look into my mother's eyes, I saw the answer. The words she spoke rolled over me like a flogging with rocks. "Chris, we will find them a good home." I knew it was coming, but hearing those words stuck a knife into my soul. I was angry, sad, and now helpless and hopeless about the future of my world and for my best friend, the one I'd leaned on all these years. The dream that had come true was now crumbling. And the feeling of helplessness was simply overwhelming.

Our pedigree horses were sold quickly to a good home. I had wished they would take Dandy too, as they seemed like such nice people. The advertisement in the paper, just like the one we had answered to buy my best friend, continued to run. My favorite goat was sold at the fair, and that heartbreak was almost all I could handle. Now I waited for the outcome for Dandy.

It was horrible to watch animals get sold off in groups, but the morning I'd really dreaded finally came. One Saturday morning, a man showed up with a stock trailer. He didn't bring his daughter or anyone to look at Dandy with him. He was strictly there for business. He and my mom talked swiftly. I stayed inside, as I just could not bear to witness what was about to happen. I felt a horrible pang in my gut, and I shook from nerves. I had seen men like this at the auction. They were liquidators. They took the unloved and unwanted animals that others sold cheap, and they sold them at auction. A lot of the horses who came through ended up on the slaughter trucks. This was the worst scenario my little brain could imagine.

The businessman decided to take some of the sheep, the ducks, and Dandy. Then the stock trailer was opened, my best friend was walked inside, and the door was closed. And at that very moment in time, my heart broke into a thousand pieces. I was forever changed on that day.

Love and every sliver of hope that I had left in me slipped away on that dirt road as the trailer drove out of sight. The little girl left behind would have scars as deep as you can imagine from that day forward.

Fighting for Milagro

KEITH LEFT TO DRIVE one of our cars up to San Diego. He was going to be gone for four days. The ladies from the barn had arranged a going-away party for me at Fran's house. I was excited but also felt a sense of sadness in leaving this incredible group of women. They had invited me into their private club, and I was so grateful. If it hadn't been for them, this would never have happened. I was grateful on Milagro's behalf and my own. We both owed a great deal to these three women.

We sat and talked on Fran's newly remodeled patio, drinking wine. Elizabeth knew that I had not committed to taking Milagro. I had gone through the motions of trying to find someone to ride him in Cabo in my absence, but that idea wasn't good for Milagro or for me. Elizabeth also knew the challenges I was facing with trying to get him up north.

As we spoke, the topic eventually came up. I think the others tried to tread lightly, as I was really broken up about the situation. I told Elizabeth, "I just wish I could take him with me." And she looked at me pointedly and said straight up in her Elizabeth way, "Well, why don't you?" In that moment, I felt her conviction and confidence in me. I had needed someone other than myself to voice these words to me. I had needed this push to help me uncover every rock or stone I could possibly move to bring Milagro home. In her straightforward, direct way, she hit a nerve in me. And it was just what I needed.

The night was wonderful. As the sun set over Pedregal and the night sky appeared, I embraced everyone in that moment. This had been a magical time, and now leaving to go home, I had a completely new determination. It was up to me to make it happen, and there would be no more waffling. The following morning when I awoke, I knew just who I needed to reach out to.

Marci had been a friend of mine for many years. She was my first client when I opened Happy Hambones Pet Sitting in San Diego around 2003. Here we were, ten-plus years later, and we still kept in touch. Marci was a dressage trainer who'd had much success in her career. Now she was living on a winery and training Azteca horses in the northern Baja area.

We kept in touch through Facebook and email. I knew that some of the horses she had trained had been sold to owners in the States. This meant they'd had to maneuver their way through the US Customs and Quarantine system. I had reached out to her on other occasions to ask her opinion on things pertaining to Milagro and his recovery. She had a world of knowledge and would be honest with me. So I sent a message and waited for her reply.

Her message was quite frank and to the point. She told me that if I was serious about getting him up to the States, she could recommend a horse transport company. She said that they were extremely conscientious and knowledgeable, and that they would get him up the Baja safely. They knew the process for quarantine and would cover that as well. Milagro would need to have his blood tested for two things to ensure he would pass quarantine. But yes, they could do it. However, it would be expensive—very expensive.

I had a few days before Keith returned home from his trip to take the car up north. He'd already expressed his feelings that this was not meant to happen. It had been a good run, and Milagro and I had a lot of fun. But it was just too big a hurdle. He didn't want to see me get my hopes up and then have them quashed. And we were partners; we made decisions together. I didn't want to strong-arm him, but I had also concluded that I was not going to let a dollar amount determine Milagro's fate. We simply had to give it our best shot.

It was Sunday, and Keith was arriving back in Cabo. I planned on picking him up at one o'clock in the afternoon. From there, he would want some beach time. His drive up had been stressful, and he would be exhausted. So after taking him home to see Roy and to unpack a bit, we threw on our suits and headed to the beach.

It was another perfect Cabo afternoon. Spring was in the air, and the warm sunshine and sparkling ocean welcomed us. We got our usual table and ordered a bucket of beer. As we sat and he unwound from his long journey, I knew that I had to talk to him. Each day was vitally important to my newly hatched plan. As much as I would have loved to give him some space, I had no choice. I had to spring it on him now.

How interesting it was that Cascadas had become the place for us to bare all. Our lengthy talks on the beach were usually full of the day-to-day things. But Cascadas had also become a place where, when we talked long enough, hidden truths came out, past hurts or disappointments. We shared celebrations of success and dreams for our future. Keith and I talked about it all. And this special beach with the quiet rhythm of the ocean had become a safe haven for us as well. This particular day was no different. Today there would be some heart-to-heart truths, and we were going to need our space to work it out. But I felt, as I always did, that our love and respect for each other was always the bottom line. And my husband would understand how much a part of me this little Baja horse had become.

Keith had a lot to take care of, so I felt guilty for putting another thing on his plate. But he loved me and he loved Milagro. My husband had the biggest heart, and I hoped he would embrace my plan.

There really was no beating around the bush. I decided to just lay it out there as simply as I could. So I did. I told him that I had come up with a way to get Milagro home with us, that I would handle all the details, and that he wouldn't have to worry about a thing. I had already arranged to have the vet come on Monday, the following morning, to draw blood and send it off to Guadalajara to be tested. I had contacted Marci and asked for the phone number of the transport company because, come hell or high water, we were not leaving Milagro behind.

I told Keith I had contacted them to find out how

much it would cost, and it was more than I had expected. And when I told him, he looked at me with that downward smile and just shook his head.

I had only a few true loves. They were Keith, Roy, Kitty, and of course Milagro. Keith tried to make some sense of the situation, and he made good points. How did we know Milagro was a sound and healthy horse? Was he strong enough to make the trip? Would he be happy there? What if we needed to move back to Cabo someday? What would we do with him up in the States?

I couldn't possibly have an answer for all of these questions. Those and others were the ones I'd had bouncing around in my head for weeks, all of the what-ifs. And the only truth that I could tell him was that I didn't know. I needed to take a leap of faith and trust that the process and the end results were meant to be.

I reminded him how, when we first met, we both had to grab hands and jump. We had to trust that what we put forth into each other would pave the road for a future, and that sometimes our only choice is to take that big leap of faith. My heart couldn't allow the alternative. I simply couldn't take another broken heart. Milagro had done something no one else could. He had reached down into my soul and pulled me up by my bootstraps. He had taken me when I was broken and shattered, lost and afraid, and he made me whole again. He turned a mirror to my soul and reminded me what I was made of. He succeeded in pulling me from the mist and making my life's path clear again. To me, it was nothing short of a miracle.

I couldn't expect anyone to understand this to the depth that I did. But after a long talk, Keith understood.

He'd seen the change in me. He knew that whatever special secret there was, Milagro had unlocked it. There just was no other way. We had to do whatever we could so that he could come with us. He belonged with us. In Mexico or across the border a thousand miles north, he belonged with us.

The conversation tempered down, and Keith agreed. He was worried about Milagro and how this would all end, but he saw a determination in me that he had never seen before. And he knew that he, too, had to take that leap of faith with me. I needed him to believe in me so that we could accomplish this together.

We laughed about how far we'd come these past several years. Recessions, hurricanes, and the loss of some of our dearest loved ones. Moving away from the security of our home. All these things had brought us to know each other more deeply, with more understanding. In that moment of his joining me in this quest, I felt immensely grateful. I'd never had someone who loved me and supported me the way he did. And I knew, now, that we were on to a very good beginning and this thing was going to happen. Now to tell Milagro the news!

The following morning, I headed to the barn to meet Dr. Fernando. She was the most qualified vet in Cabo, and she spoke fairly good English, so that was helpful. She arrived on time in a shiny new truck and was dressed sharply for a barn call. The only time I had met her previously was when she came out to do the horses' teeth. That hadn't gone all that well. Milagro had required several injections to calm him down enough to get his teeth done, and the whole thing had been a bit traumatic. But

I expected today to be simple, as all we needed to do was draw some blood and then get it shipped off to the laboratory in Guadalajara.

The blood draw went fine. And Dr. Fernando told me she would send the blood to the lab and we could expect results in seven to nine days. I explained to her that I had fifteen days to make arrangements and that Milagro would need to be shipped out before we left on the first of the month. She assured me the results would come back to us within the seven to nine days. And at that point, we would know for sure if he was able to pass inspections at quarantine. By getting those results in the time frame we expected, I could then give the go-ahead for the transport company to begin their way down the Baja to pick up Milagro.

Daniela at the transport company was very helpful. She did speak English but not as well as I would have liked. The company clearly had years of experience with moving horses all around Mexico, the US, and Canada. But I was new to this and had a lot of questions. With our language barrier, it was hard to get those concerns across to Daniela. I told her in the best way I could that we had to wait until I got the results back from the lab in Guadalajara before anyone should drive down the Baja to pick him up. Without the proper results from the lab, there would be no sending Milagro up north. She seemed to get this point, and with that, I left it alone.

Daniela and Keith spoke on occasion as well. He helped make sure the paperwork they needed was signed and ready for them. And he made the arrangements for them to receive payment. During one conversation in particular, I overheard him say something pertaining to Milagro being a pet. As he was speaking in Spanish, I didn't know exactly what they were talking about, so when he hung up, I asked him. Keith laughed and told me Daniela had asked him, "So what kind of racehorse is he?" "Racehorse? He's no racehorse!" Keith had replied. "He's my wife's pet." And then he'd let out a hearty laugh. This was the first time they had been asked to drive all the way down the Baja to Land's End for a horse, and they just assumed it was a racehorse. No, no racehorse, but a very special horse at that. And they would be making this journey solely for Milagro.

Dr. Fernando had been good to explain to me that once we got the results, there would be other hurdles to cross. She told me that the governmental agricultural department would need to make a physical inspection of Milagro to clear him of any ticks or other transferable pests or diseases. This would turn out to be a very critical examination, as the paperwork they would give to me would only be good for three days. Milagro would have to get to the border and cross inspections in Mexico within three days or their paperwork would no longer apply. So now we needed to wait for the bloodwork to come back, arrange for the inspections to take place, and ensure that the transport company would arrive in Cabo and get him back up the border before that paperwork expired. This was stressing me out. I was already anxious enough about the timing of the transport company with the blood results, on top of our flight leaving on May 1. I was packing and finalizing things at our house along with getting the proper paperwork to bring Roy and Kitty up with us on the plane. My stomach was constantly in knots. And adding to the stress, we were not receiving the blood test results back as promised.

It had been seven days and nothing from Dr. Fernando. I tried not to be pushy, as that did not bode well in Mexico. They didn't see why we Americans got so uptight over things, and they tended to push back. On day nine, I texted her and asked about the results. Still nothing from the lab in Guadalajara. I was a mess.

On the eleventh day, she called me and I was so excited, certain she had the results. But no, she was calling to tell me that she had recently learned I would need yet another important document from the municipality in San José. I was so angry I couldn't see straight. Did she not understand the importance of all this? Did she not see how urgent this all was and how much I was relying on her? She was so nonchalant about the whole thing that I wanted to scream. But I couldn't. I had to stay calm and play her game of cat and mouse. What did she want from me? Money? Yes, but she wasn't good at extortion. If she would only state her price, I would be happy to oblige. But I realized this was more than an opportunity to screw me; she truly didn't care whether Milagro left Cabo at all. She didn't believe in us; she didn't believe in me. And that infuriated me to no end. We had come so very far, and to have this gal playing with the fate of my horse was excruciating.

On day twelve, I continued with the plan for inspection. Saul had been so kind to make Milagro shine like a new penny. He'd been thoroughly bathed with an analgesic shampoo I bought especially for ticks. We all knew he didn't have a single tick, and Saul was offended at the thought any of his horses would carry ticks. But he also knew the game I had to play, and he, along with everyone else at our little barn, was rooting for Milagro. Saul clipped all the hair from his ears and patted them down with the white powder that would tell the inspectors he'd been treated for pests. His legs were cleanly shaven and his sheath cleaned. He looked amazing, and as Saul took him from his stall to ready him, the agricultural department arrived.

In Mexico they love their paperwork and their sense of authority. The two men who arrived were dressed in slacks, button-down shirts, belts, and leather loafers. One of them carried a briefcase. This was Saul's territory, so I stood back and didn't say a word. I think I actually held my breath for part of the time. But then I would look at Milagro and remind myself how far he had come. I looked into his eyes as he watched these guys go over him. He looked at me as if to say "Don't worry, we got this." And as helpless as I felt, I just had to keep on believing in him.

The inspection went quickly, and then they handed me a piece of paper and told me it would cost 250 pesos. I got out my pesos to pay them, and they started to chuckle. Saul quickly interceded and directed me to *el banco*. Turned out, I had to go to the bank, pay for the document to be processed, and then return with a receipt showing I had paid—and then they could hand over the necessary documents. Saul and Milagro shooed me off to my car to go take care of this little bit of business. I drove fast, waited outside the bank until it opened, and worried they would leave if I didn't get back to the barn in time.

I was the first in line at *el banco* and paid the fee, got

it stamped and triple stamped, and drove back to the barn as fast as I could. There, the men waited and handed me my paperwork. During the time I was gone, Saul had shared with them just a bit of Milagro's history. I could tell now that these kind men understood what I was trying to do. And they respected me for it. They, too, were on Milagro's side.

As they handed me the papers, I felt so relieved. This one big hurdle had been completed. It was a good sign and gave me the confidence I needed to push through these next few days. I called Dr. Fernando and told her I had gotten the inspection. She said she was working on getting the other paper I would need but still hadn't gotten the blood tests back. I don't think I even heard her. I just reveled in this one big win for our team and didn't feed into her game. I had to keep the faith.

On day thirteen, it had been almost two weeks since Dr. Fernando came out to take Milagro's blood, assuring me that we'd have results within seven to nine days. She had no good excuse for not getting the results. And she didn't seem to care one way or the other. It was around noon, and I had gone home from the office to have lunch. As I sat eating my sandwich, with Roy by my side, my phone rang. I leapt off the couch and ran to the phone. I saw that it was Keith and my heart sank. I had hoped it would be Dr. Fernando. I answered the phone, thinking it was nothing too important, and Keith told me, "Your driver is here." "What driver?" I asked. "The driver to pick up Milagro, he's at the Walmart parking lot." "Here in Cabo?" I asked. It couldn't be. I hadn't given them the go-ahead yet. "Well he is here and wants to go drop off his trailer at the barn. He plans on sleeping over tonight and then leaving with Milagro in the morning."

What had just happened? I had been telling Daniela that we didn't have the results yet and that they needed to wait. She knew our deadline for getting out of here was the fourteenth. Somehow we must have crossed wires, because I was under the impression they would not leave Tijuana until I gave the go-ahead. Keith put me in touch with the driver via text. And we agreed to meet out at the barn. And then I called Dr. Fernando.

I was no longer able to hold in my emotions at this point. This entire process had been so hard on us all. She answered and I flatly told her, "You need to get those results NOW. My driver is here, in Cabo, and he is going to take Milagro. You need to get those results NOW." And in her usual manner, she danced around with no real substantial information. She told me she would call the lab and check to see if they had them in yet.

A short time later, I got a text from Dr. Fernando. She said that she hoped they would have them by the end of the day but that she would prepare her paperwork and get it ready. This was the first sign she was bending in our direction. She said she needed a copy of the transport driver's license so that she could put it on the paperwork. Whatever, one more ridiculous hoop to jump through. So I texted the driver, whose name was Juan Pablo. I had not met Juan yet, as we were going to meet at the barn shortly. He quickly did as I asked and sent me a photo of his license.

The picture was of a strong, thick, sturdy-looking man, older and mature with a big neck and balding head.

He looked like a man I wouldn't want to mess with. And apparently he had the top class of driver's license possible in the country of Mexico. I had learned how classist Mexico was while living there. And Juan Pablo's credentials spoke volumes. The fact that he had come down from Tijuana added a bit of intrigue to him as well. So when I texted the image to Dr. Fernando, it was a turning point.

Within ten minutes of me sending that picture, Dr. Fernando was doing backflips to get me the paperwork. She said that she had just heard back from the lab, that Milagro was clear for both tests, and that he would, in fact, pass inspection at quarantine. She told me that I could come to her vet clinic and pick up the paperwork in about an hour. "And what about that last piece of paperwork we need from San José?" I asked. "Oh, that is not necessary. You will have what you need. Come to the clinic in one hour and I will have it for you."

As relieved and exuberant as I felt, I was also mystified by how this had all suddenly changed with the good Dr. Fernando. Was it the driver being here that lit a fire under her ass? Or was it the fact that the driver was a Class A driver from Tijuana who had been hired by these gringos to pick up this non-pedigree horse? I think Dr. Fernando's imagination got the best of her and she decided not to play games with me anymore. She decided not to tango with Juan Pablo.

I drove into the *barrio* and parked outside the vet clinic. I had been here before to pick up a thing or two for Milagro. It was around the corner from our little feed store. As I waited in the lobby, I could not wipe the smile from my face. As much as I had enjoyed this adventure, it was time to go home. Mexico has a way of testing me, and this one final test had me just about at my breaking point. But here I was, about to get the documents I so desperately needed to make our dream come true.

Dr. Fernando could not have been more polite. She thanked me and even waived the fee for the paperwork because it took so long. I didn't hold anything against her. Whatever really happened, or whatever her real plan was to extort money from me at the final moments, I had let it go. Because in the end, we had what we needed, and that was all I could think of in that moment. And I knew that I would never again be subjected to this kind of mind game. Because not only were we all going back to the States, but we were taking Milagro with us.

I left the vet clinic and drove out towards the barn. I was scheduled to meet up with Juan Pablo so that he could drop off the trailer. He met me out front and was talking with Saul when I arrived.

I hadn't had time to even question why he came down before I signaled the green light. The past few hours had my head spinning every which way. But here he was, just a man on a mission, with no clue as to the fretting and stress I had been through. And as it turned out, this little mess-up had been one of the best things to happen. I wanted to hug him and tell him thank you—thank you for arriving today and for whatever miracles you brought with you. But I kept myself in check and just smiled and told him how very happy I was to see him.

Juan Pablo had brought along an apprentice driver as well. This way, they could take breaks driving up the Baja and get across those checkpoints in time—another fantastic bit of news, as they only had two days to complete the drive. Saul was thrilled that this was all coming together. He tried to hide his excitement, but I could read his face. We were all equally thrilled with the arrival of Juan Pablo and his helper.

We all agreed to meet at nine o'clock the following morning. This would give Milagro time to finish his breakfast before they got on the road. I had never taken him anywhere in a horse trailer. Besides his being brought to Saul's by Elizabeth when she rescued him, I had no idea if he'd ever ridden in one. But I knew Milagro, and he was a strong horse with a level head—he would do just fine.

On day fourteen, I stopped by the office to pick up Keith, and we headed to the barn. It was a beautiful spring morning. Not too hot, not too cold—just right. Juan Pablo was there when we arrived, and the trailer was open. He had laid down fresh shavings and was busy loading their water tank with water from the barn. It was vitally important for Milagro to drink ample water on the journey, so bringing water that he was familiar with made it more likely that he would do just that. A hay net was loaded with fresh green alfalfa. Everything had been thought of and was in place and ready for Milagro's journey. One horse, two drivers, and a thousand long and winding miles to cover.

I handed Juan the vitally important paperwork I had received from Dr. Fernando. He seemed more interested in the agricultural inspection paperwork, as this was what he needed to pass the checkpoints up the Baja. The all-important bloodwork that had created such a stress was now pushed to the back. Milagro would be tested again at the border, but this paperwork meant we knew he would pass. It didn't do a thing, though, for the task at hand, which was driving from Land's End to Tijuana.

So we all watched as Saul took Milagro from his stall one last time. He gave him a pat on the neck, smiled, and then handed the lead rope to Juan Pablo. I could tell that Juan had a way with horses. He was a strong, steady, and gentle man, the kind of person a horse sees as a good leader. He took the lead and walked Milagro down the corridor past all his friends. I watched and waited for a hesitation, perhaps. Milagro wasn't a fan of leaving the barn by himself, as this was the only real home he'd ever known. But on this morning, something was different. I believe he knew exactly what was happening. He had been listening to me all this time, telling him about this day, and here we were. He knew he had been prepped for his journey. And he was ready.

Milagro walked strong and steady, with his head held high. He carried himself in a poised manner as he passed his friends Carlos, Apollo, and Fran's horse, Toby. He didn't hesitate one bit, and if anything, he walked with a proud determination. Juan Pablo led him out towards the gate, and we all gathered and followed behind. He then walked Milagro up to the trailer, and with one quick sniff, he stepped inside and right on up to the hay net. Juan tied him so that he could move his head about as necessary. And then he closed up the back of the huge trailer. Milagro looked so small in there all by himself. But he was ready. I could see it in his eyes: He knew something special was happening, and he was ready.

We shook hands with everyone and watched as Juan Pablo and his junior driver took their seats. It took a few attempts to get the large truck and trailer turned around. He was a professional with a big job ahead and was all business. Keith and I, Saul and Fran, we all watched as

Juan Pablo slowly pulled out and up the road, made the turn, and headed out on the main road. I hugged Saul and thanked him for all he had done for Milagro, all he had done for us. Fran just smiled, put her hands in the air, and said, "Good luck!"

Keith and I jumped in our car and drove alongside them for a few miles until they took the turn north towards Todos Santos. I had tears streaming down my cheeks, and I waved at them. Keith took my hand and squeezed it hard, and I could feel it was hot and clammy. He, too, was overwhelmed with emotions. We looked at each other, and he said, "You know you're crazy." And I said, "Yes, and that's why you love me." He just smiled and shook his head, and we both knew that this was a day we would never forget.

Reflection

I WANTED TO SAVOR THIS MOMENT and freeze it in time. I had accomplished something no one thought I could, and now Milagro was on his way to the USA. But there was no time to relish in the glory, as we had a lot to get done before our flight the following day. My heart had swelled with gratitude, but my head was screaming at me to get focused. There was no time for such things. There was still plenty to do to pack up the house and to get Roy and Kitty ready for their adventure to the US the following day. So Keith dropped me off at home to get started, and he headed back to the office. He, too, had plenty to get done before we left the following day.

Roy and Kitty would be making the short flight back to San Diego. I packed all their things in Roy's crate, which was now playing the part of the pets' suitcase. Kitty's litter box, food, bowls, and toys as well as Roy's memory-foam dog bed and his things were crammed into the crate. I made sure Keith and I were packed with enough clothing and belongings for ten days, as he was also going to make a return trip to drive up the last car within that time frame. We'd rented a furnished condo in San Diego, giving us time to find long-term housing.

The plan seemed easy and efficient, but traveling with two animals, and a third on his way, had me in fits. But by the end of the day, as the sun set on the Pacific, I began to savor what was happening. After all those times I had thought about leaving Mexico, and how happy I would be to see it in the rearview mirror, now I didn't feel the same way. The four years here had left me a changed person. It was bittersweet, and as Keith and I walked to the beach with Roy one last time, I fully grasped the incredible experience for what it was and what it had done for me. I felt so much gratitude that day, not only for finding Milagro a way home with us but for my entire experience here. I could not have planned or experienced it any better. It would be hard to share it with or explain it to others, and that in itself made it that much more sacred. It was so powerful to sense real growth within myself, and I had grown plenty. My marriage, the way I viewed life and others, were far different, and I had Mexico to thank

CHRISTIE BONHAM   145

for that. So, no, I was not going to shed tears of joy for leaving, as I'd once thought I would. I was shedding tears of joy for what I was taking with me. The lessons I had learned here were worth more than I could imagine.

The next day came fast, and the shuttle arrived to pick us all up. Roy jumped in, parked himself by a window, and looked out with a gaze of enchantment. I wondered if he knew he was leaving this wonderland and never coming back. Could he read that from me, or was he just out taking a joyride? Whatever it was, he seemed unfazed. Keith was quiet and seemed to be in deep thought as well. He had weathered some big storms and carried a lot of the responsibility for us in making this a good journey. He had done a great job, and we had worked hard and held it together through some of the more rocky times. In the end, it had bonded us in a much deeper way, and I understood my husband in ways I never could have without these past four years. He was always one to focus on the future because, as the saying goes, "the view is much greater through the windshield than in the rearview mirror." He wasn't one to get emotional, but I knew it had meant so much to him as well.

The airport was fairly quiet, and we checked in without any problems. Once inside, we sat down at the food court. There was fake turf that covered the floors, so it was a nice, comfortable place for Roy to rest before we boarded our flight. I watched the people around us, all tan and happy from their time here in Cabo. And I thought about those arriving. Some would be coming for a short vacation, but others may be starting their journey on a deeper level. I wondered what experiences those newcomers would have. What would they take away with

Last Christmas in Cabo

them at the end of their journey? Or would they stay? I had met people who came to Cabo many years before me and never left. They found a place in the world that fit them best, and they decided to plant roots.

Cabo has a way of getting into your blood, and before you know it, there you are, growing along with the *choyero*. There is a saying that if you have been in Cabo long enough, you're given the nickname "choyero," as this cactus grows burrs that get attached to livestock who carry it a far, far distance until the *choyero* drops and falls to the ground. And there it begins to grow roots and start all over again.

After a cold *cerveza*, we waited until it was time to board our flight. Just like the flight coming here four years ago, this was a one-way ticket. It was back to our homeland, where our family waited and where Milagro would soon be arriving, back to the familiar rules and lifestyle that had been mine for much of my life, away from this new life I had grown to love. It was bittersweet.

Milagro's Journey

AS WE WERE MAKING OUR WAY to San Diego, so was Milagro. He had left just one day ahead of us. The following day, I received a text that said he had made it all the way up the Baja safely. He would be spending two days at the famous Caliente Racetrack in Tijuana to rest. And from there, he would be loaded up once again to travel six hours east to Yuma, Arizona, where the US Customs had their quarantine.

Daniela sent me a picture of Milagro in his box stall at the Caliente Racetrack. He had his head sticking out over the Dutch door, and his face had an inquisitive expression. He looked good and didn't seem to be showing the signs of stress I had worried about. No doubt the long journey had been hard on him. But he looked as though he was keeping his spirits high.

I thought about all the famous racehorses who had come before him to stay in his box stall: from the likes of Phar Lap, the Australian racehorse who traveled great distances to race in a world-class event, only to die at Caliente and never return to his home country; to Seabiscuit, whose time on the track united our country; and ignited a newfound determination after the Great Depression—all the winners and all the losers who had crossed through that place in an effort to carve out a name for themselves. Milagro was not a racehorse, and luckily for him, there was nothing to prove. But Caliente was part of one of the biggest challenges of his life, and that was making it unscathed up and over the border. This first journey and his few days of rest would soon be behind him. I was comforted by his picture but also knew he still had a great deal of work ahead of him.

We had arrived in San Diego and were getting settled into our short-term living accommodations as quickly as we could. Having only brought enough clothes for a couple of weeks made it easy to unpack. Roy and Kitty had their favorites things placed about in our new condo. Roy's large dog bed, his toys, and his food and water bowls were in easy-to-find locations. He seemed to be enjoying this new adventure and adapted quite well to taking the elevator from our second-story location to the ground level for his walks. Meeting new people and their pets in this lively urban environment put a new skip in his step. Kitty was enjoying exploring the three stories full of new furniture to jump onto and places to run and play hide-and-seek. It was easy to settle in.

Keith only spent a few days in San Diego before he flew back down to Cabo. He was about to embark on his last and final leg of the move, which was to pack up all the loose ends in his large SUV and drive it up the Baja. He had already driven my Jeep up weeks earlier. That drive compounded with the flight and move into our short-term place had left him drained. I was worried about him. Making that drive alone once was a lot to handle, but he had one more trip to make. How long would it be before we were all together again? This move was proving to take its toll on us all. But Keith and Milagro were bearing the brunt of it.

The day Keith flew back, I received another text from Daniela. She told me that Milagro had made the drive to the quarantine at the US Customs office in Yuma. This was good news. Two legs of the journey were now behind him. There, he would stay up to four days while officers took his blood and ran lab tests to ensure that he was healthy and fit to cross into the US. I knew that he had been tested for these same diseases by Dr. Fernando in Cabo. These were the test results that had created such stress leading up to his departure from Cabo, the results that finally came in on the last possible day for Milagro to make his journey north, and they had been good results. But I still worried that somehow those findings may have been wrong, that perhaps Milagro would test positive on this second round of labs. And then what on earth was I going to do?

The next few days were long and full of anxiety. I was in San Diego, trying to get some sort of new routine in place. Keith was going to be gone another five days with his final cleanup of our house and then the drive north. And Milagro was in some unknown quarantine isolation yard on the Mexican border in Arizona. He had been through so much already that I wondered if he was losing his faith in me. I had told him that it would be a long and difficult journey and that he would need his strength. And I knew he heard me, and he believed in me. I just hoped he would keep that faith a little while longer. The drive had surely taken a toll on his strength and physical well-being. I hoped his mind was still in a good place.

Each day went by without a word from Daniela. At this point, Milagro was in the hands of the US government. I trusted that they were caring for him in a compassionate manner. I knew they had set standards to keep, which included food, water, and necessary veterinary attention if warranted. But I could not speak to someone to ask them how my horse was doing. And they were not going to send any text messages with cute pictures of Milagro. I had been cut off, and I was at the mercy of the laboratory results once more. Damn these blood tests. And until they came in, I wasn't getting my Milagro back to the states.

It was a rainy Friday, and I woke up to check my phone. No messages from Daniela. My heart sank. I brewed a pot of coffee and quickly dressed to take Roy out for his walk. The clouds and rain made for a fast lap, and soon Roy and I were back inside. As he ate his breakfast, I heard my phone buzz with an incoming text message. I dodged over Kitty to grab my phone and saw that it was from Daniela. I wrestled with my readers to get them on so that I could read her message. And it said that they had received clearance for Milagro and that he would be crossing the border that day. She told me that the driver would call me as he got closer, to arrange for the time of delivering Milagro, and that I should make sure to be near the phone when he called. Oh, hallelujah, I could not believe my eyes! Today was the day my Milagro would be entering his new life, and by the end of today, I would have him back in my care. I hugged myself and jumped up and down with cheers. Roy danced around my feet and wagged his tail in delight. Whatever the cause for delight, Roy was thrilled to be a part of it. With no one else in sight to share my happiness, I hugged him too.

I called Keith in Cabo to tell him the good news right away. I knew he had been holding his breath, just as I had been, waiting to hear this news. He answered the phone, and I could tell he was in a rush. But as I blurted out that Milagro was finally going to make it to his new home today, Keith's spirits lifted and he let out a heavy sigh. He was happy for me, and he was thrilled for Milagro. Yes, finally this little red Mexican pony would make his way home to be with us.

I hung up with Keith and called the manager at the new boarding facility where I had decided to keep Milagro. The Double D had been a recommendation from my friend Marci, who had recommended the transportation company that was now driving Milagro to his new home in San Diego. Her recommendation along with my own history with Lakeside made it a perfect choice for Milagro—this was the area where I grew up riding Dandy. My family had lived in Lakeside all those years ago, and it felt like I was making a loop back to those earlier happy times of my youth. It had a comfort and familiarity to it that I just knew would make it a good place for Milagro and me to start over together.

The stable was large, with over eighty horses. The facility was laid out in the shape of a horseshoe, with large riding arenas in the front and smaller turnout pens in the back. All the horses were in 24 x 24 pipe corrals with a 12 x 12 shelter. They each had an electric waterer and feedings came twice a day, with the pens cleaned daily. It was much larger than our small barn in Cabo with just twelve horses. Moving from such a small and comfortable environment to one with so much going on at once could be a bit overwhelming, but I knew with time we would find our place there.

I called the Double D and told them the driver would be calling me when he was closer and we could plan on meeting there in the late afternoon. I had an invitation to my sister Cindy's home that evening for a baby shower. They lived only ten minutes from the Double D, so I thought I could attend the shower and, when the call came from the driver, I could make a quick exit to go directly to the barn. Everything was falling into place.

The rain continued to come down that day, light but steady. I was worried about the driver making his way through the desert and up and over the pass with the bad road conditions, but I kept my mind from wandering too far into the space of worry. The wait had gone from days to hours now. Milagro's journey was about to come to an end.

I arrived at my sister's house and told her I would be leaving abruptly, and explained why. They also knew about my horse coming to the States, and they were all cheering for him. Everyone shared their excitement, and it made me feel so comforted. All these people from different parts of my life were aware of this undertaking, and they all secretly cheered for Milagro's successful arrival.

The call came in, and as the driver told me in his broken English that he was twenty minutes away, my heart started beating faster and faster. After I excused myself from the baby shower, I jumped in my car to head to the barn. There were two ways I could drive there. The route on the highway might take a bit longer, or I could take the back roads and probably save some time. I chose to take the back roads, as in that moment, I could barely stand the suspense.

I made my way through the back roads and came to the intersection that crossed the highway. As I waited for the light to turn green, I watched a large dually truck towing a large horse trailer pass through the intersection before me. The truck had its safety lights on and was moving cautiously on the wet roads. As I watched it pass in front of me, I recognized it as the truck that had come to Cabo to pick up Milagro. It was painted blue with large white stripes, so I was sure it was the truck. The trailer was different and much larger than the one used to load Milagro up when he left Cabo. But I was certain that this was the driver, and that inside this new, fancier version of a trailer was my boy!

The light turned green, and I drove quickly to catch up to the truck and trailer. Only a couple miles left until we got to the Double D, I thought about how incredible it was that I could give them a personalized escort to the ranch. I caught up to the truck, slowed to his speed, and also turned on my safety flashers. There was no taking chances with this precious cargo.

The driver put on his right blinker to turn onto the

driveway of the Double D. The rain began to lighten and came to a complete stop. There was quietness in the air, and the barn was empty of people except for the barn managers. They had been waiting in the office, and when we pulled up, they came out quickly.

The driver slowly parked his rig and jumped out, grabbing a set of gloves and a lead rope. I could see now that there were a total of six horses in the trailer, and by the looks of them, they were all large show horses. Big heads with large necks and full forelocks peered out over their hay nets through the windows. I looked for Milagro but did not see his face.

Pablo, the driver, greeted me and then opened up the back of the trailer and put down the ramp. As soon as he had opened the door, I looked inside, and there he was; Milagro was at the end of the trailer, as he was the first to be delivered. Pablo gave him a pat on his neck and then tied a lead rope to his halter and led him out of the trailer.

So much emotion had built up inside me that I didn't know what to feel first. I was thrilled beyond imagination to see him again. I could hardly believe that he was standing there right before my eyes. I wanted to hug him and kiss his face! I spoke to him to try to soothe him. I had been so worried about how the trip would affect him. People warned me he would lose weight and it would be stressful. I also knew that he could recover quickly with the proper attention. Right now, I just wanted to comfort him and celebrate this moment of his arrival.

I spoke to Pablo and thanked him for his special care of this very special horse. He smiled a crooked grin, and I could tell through our unspoken language that he understood this horse meant the world to me. I doubted he would have many opportunities to make someone's dreams come true. And I believe, in that moment, he felt it was an honor to have fulfilled mine. I shook his hand, looked into his eyes, smiled, and thanked him.

I took the lead from Pablo, held Milagro, and let him sniff the ground. I walked him in slow circles to ease his angst. Milagro was so tired and somewhat amiss as to what he had been going through. His eyes were large, and he was breathing somewhat fast. I could tell that this had been rough on him. I was happy that he could now rest. He was home. He had done his part and kept the faith and stayed strong, and it was now time to rest.

I led him slowly around the property and then to his stall. Inside the stall was a fresh flake of hay and water. I removed his halter and saw rub marks on the side of his face from where the halter had rubbed off some of his hair. A long time in a trailer was certain to take its toll. But after a full inspection, I felt relieved that this, along with only a slight weight loss, was the worst of it. We could overcome that together in the coming months.

The managers stayed around a bit, then bid their farewell. They had work to tend to, and I think they could tell I wanted to spend some quiet time alone with Milagro. I shook their hands, and they gave Milagro a quick pat on the neck.

As I sat alone against the corral, I watched Milagro move about slowly in his stall. He sniffed the ground and poked his head up to listen to the new sounds and take in the new smells in this foreign land. His breathing started to slow, and he took nibbles of the fresh alfalfa. The air was cool and misty from the rain. I was sure this was all new for him, being a boy from the tropics. He eventually

Milagro meets the family

came to me and stood right in front of me, asking for attention. I told him what a good boy he was and how happy I was to have him here. His ears pricked forward as I whispered to him, "You see, we did it." And with that, he let out a long heavy breath and shook his head up and down. Yes, he said, we did it.

Vet Check

OVER THE NEXT FEW DAYS, I visited Milagro at the barn each day. We walked around the property and got to know some of the other boarders and their horses. Milagro was eating well, and aside from the minor weight loss, he was in good spirits. One of the first things I wanted to do once we settled in was to have a proper vet check. Having access to the vet care provided in the States was something I was excited about, and I was really curious to learn what they would have to say about Milagro.

Dr. Joleen was the vet who handled almost all the horses at the Double D. She came highly recommended, so I contacted her for an appointment. About a week after Milagro's arrival, we met out at the ranch. I introduced her to Milagro and shared his story with her. Because she was a kind and intuitive person, she was very moved by what he had been through—his life's struggles, rescue, and rehabilitation, and then his journey to America. I showed her a few before-and-after pictures of Milagro. She was absolutely shocked that he had made such a recovery without any medical intervention. As she put it, "This horse was ten days or so away from death. Horses in that condition rarely make a full recovery even with all the best the medical world can offer. The fact that he did it with only food, water, and love—it's a miracle."

"Yes," I said, "it certainly is."

She first started by giving him a good look over. She said that, considering what we knew of his age and how much neglect he had seen in his life, he was sound and without any noticeable physical limitations. This was not to discount the road map of scars he had on his body that told of a different story. But Milagro was in good health. She was the first to tell me what she thought his origin to be. I had always thought of Milagro as some blending of breeds without any particular attribute. But she told me she thought he was a Spanish Colonial horse, the breed of horse that Christopher Columbus brought with him to the Americas and that the Spanish conquistadors rode in their marking of their new land. What a wonderful thing to hear! Milagro's gait, his conformation, and his small stature all pointed in this direction. Not to mention, herds of these horses had continued to be bred just the way they were for many years in Mexico. It helped me to understand him even more. His lineage of strength had endured for centuries. There was no sure way of knowing this, though, since we could never find out who his parents were and if they had any pedigree. But that didn't matter to me. Either way, he was always the warrior inside that I thought him to be.

Dr. Joleen and I discussed the obvious, which was Milagro's continued need to gain weight and good muscle. Although he had made a miraculous recovery back when he was at Saul's in Cabo, he still needed that valuable muscle mass that could take years to redevelop. The feed in Cabo had been good enough, but now that we were in the land of plenty, we could do more. We discussed this for a while and determined that it would be a good idea to get him on a new diet, including lunch and some extra grain and supplements to help him achieve this goal. This would take a few months, and his body was going to change.

I told her I would be shopping for a new saddle, as the old one was a poor fit, and Dr. Joleen suggested I give him some time off to let him gain weight. Then we could start looking to fit a saddle since his body conformation would change, as would the fit of the saddle. This all sounded like a reasonable plan to me. I thought he would enjoy taking the hiatus and getting to live the high life of good food, lots of rest, and spoils from me. I didn't realize that, for Milagro, not working was a dangerous thing, for in the past, during the longest summer, when he stopped working altogether, he also stopped eating and drinking, and it all became unbearable.

Finding Our New Home

KEITH WAS CONTINUING TO TRAVEL back and forth to Mexico for work as I was trying to settle us into life back in the States. The stress of the move and our ever-changing home life was taking its toll on my health in little ways. Although it was a reprieve to be out of the heat and humidity of the Baja, I was struggling with fatigue, and my body wasn't able to sustain a lot at once. Overdoing it only brought on an exasperation of the all-too-familiar tweaks my body showed to communicate its resignation and protest. Taking breaks and sneaking in naps as needed were happening more frequently. It was hard to focus on finding us a new home. I wanted so much to reconnect with my friends and family, but it was a lot to do at once. So I focused on taking on daily tasks in small bites, always giving myself a buffer of time around them to recharge as needed. I had an appointment with Dr. Peters scheduled for the summertime. But I was learning to listen to my body, and for now, it needed to take it slow and steady.

We were living in a furnished condo in downtown San Diego. We gave ourselves two months in this place so that I could focus on finding the right home. Having a big dog like Roy, plus a cat, would make finding a rental home more difficult. San Diego is a very competitive market where you have to be ready to jump on a house immediately if you're interested in it. I was pretty consumed by caring for our aging dog, driving out to care for Milagro in his new surroundings, and looking for a new home for us. I was scattered about, and it seemed I wasn't doing any one thing very well. But I was trying.

Soon I found a house for us to rent. That meant it was time to finally move from the temporary condo to our new home. Everything had to be brought in from storage, and it took time to unpack and get settled.

Settling In

ALSO THROWN INTO THIS MIX were our parents. My mom, who had been living at a memory care facility for the past two years, suddenly needed to be moved. The place where she had been living was sold to a larger company, and they were restructuring it in a way that didn't meet her needs any longer. We had a tight budget to work with, and it was not easy to find a new suitable place for her.

Plus, Keith's dad was getting ready to have his first of two hip replacement surgeries. Keith's mother had been holding on to things that should have been tossed out long ago, so his father needed help clearing out the house so he could come home and navigate around without running into things. With each and every item having some meaning to her, this was a tiresome and lengthy process.

All the while, I kept my routine and made it out to see Milagro. For the first month or so, he seemed to be pretty happy with his newfound rest-and-relaxation program. But it wasn't too long into this that I started noticing angst in him. He was beginning to spook while we went on our walks around the stable. He seemed hotheaded and anxious in ways I had not seen him before. I took it to mean the extra food we were giving him might be making him feel frisky. But it didn't seem right.

July rolled around and we had finally gotten our home set up. We had fortunately found a place for Mom as well, and it turned out to be within five miles of where Milagro lived. It was a lovely home for women only, with about twelve residents, and Mom seemed to settle in rather quickly, which made us all feel relieved. The day I drove her there and took her inside to her room, she smiled and her eyes were wide with excitement. She watched proudly as my brother, his wife, my nephew, and I all took turns bringing in piles of her things. We set up her bed and put away her clothes. It was a corner room and had a lovely view of the palapa and palm trees in the backyard. I realized that this looked a lot like her old house, which she must have found comforting. She wasn't able to communicate much anymore, but we could all see she was curious about, and content with, these new surroundings, not scared or worried.

The following day, I came to visit her on my way to see Milagro. I walked into her room, where they were dressing her for the day. She was suddenly all chatty, and as her eyes widened with excitement, she said to me, "We climbed to the top of the mountain and got to the other side together." I wasn't exactly sure where this was coming from, but the overall sentiment was that she had taken a journey and had finally made it to her destination, and she was quite all right with that. How ironic that I, too, had just taken quite a journey and made it to the other side, I thought. I looked at her, held her hand, and agreed that, yes, we had made it to the top of the mountain, together.

I soon found that the location of her new home was very convenient. Not only was I able to stop by and see her much more freely since she and Milagro were so close to one another, but the fact that she was now just one stop off the road on my way to see Milagro made the choice less complicated. It's hard to see a parent in the conditions of late Alzheimer's. But I found that the more often I visited, the more likely I was to get a moment with her when she had clarity. It was a roll of the dice. One day, it was gray and hazy. The next, it was like the wind had swept the air clean and her thoughts were lucid and clear. I never had expectations. I just gave us the chance, and to my surprise, on more days than not, my mother was there.

We had finally gotten my in-laws' home cleared out as much as possible. My father-in-law was on the schedule for his hip replacement in a few weeks. Everything seemed to be settling down. And then I got a call from my brother Tony.

Dad's Health

I HAVE TWO BROTHERS. TONY is the oldest and is five years older than me, and Michael is our middle brother. While we'd all been close over the years, lately there had been tension between us regarding our mom. Families don't always agree on the best way to address an aging parent, and as it turned out, Mike and I had different ideas when it pertained to our mother. It had gotten bad. And while I was still living in Cabo, the three of us were having a conference call about our mom one night, and Mike and I got into a quarrel that did not end well. Even with Tony's levelheadedness trying to hold the three of us together, I had blown.

So when Tony told me Mike had called him about our dad, I was concerned. Mike had told him that Dad had been having some recent issues and behavior changes he was worried about. Apparently Mike had been out to visit Dad and was alarmed at some things he was seeing, and wanted us to know about them.

Tony told me Mike was coming to his house the following day to talk about this. Mike was in town for the weekend, and it was a good opportunity to sit down and discuss it. He invited me to come as well. My first reaction was *no*. But I later changed my mind. Although our family had its share of rifts, this was not the time to be stubborn.

The following day, we met at Tony's house. I wondered how Mike would greet me, or how we would feel after our blowout about Mom, but we looked at each other and the air was cleared. It had to be. We had bigger problems at hand.

We spent the day talking about our father, who had some serious issues to face, and how to help him. We talked about our mom and how she was in a good place, and by some miracle, this change in her home had allowed us all to come to an agreement. And we talked about each other and what was going on in our lives. Keith was working in Cabo, and Vicki, Mike's wife, was not with him. Cindy, Tony's wife, was gone for most of the day, so the three of us got a chance to sit back, have some drinks, and be together, just the three of us joining forces to talk about our parents. It was a healing day for me in many ways. I am so glad we had the opportunity to mend because what came next would require us to be a united front.

Dad had been to see a doctor when Mike visited, but he was reluctant to go through with the recommended MRI and CT scan. Dad was highly claustrophobic, and the thought of doing that test worried him deeply. His symptoms were all over the place. About a week after our meeting at Tony's house, Mike got a call from Arizona that Dad was back in the hospital. He could no longer walk.

At this point, he was willing to do the recommended tests. By the end of that day, we discovered what was causing our father's drastic decline. He had a brain tumor. And he was scheduled for emergency surgery the following day.

The surgery went well, and the tumor was removed. It was biopsied and the diagnosis was not good: Stage 4 aggressive brain cancer. The doctors told us that this tumor had grown to the size of a golf ball in about three or four months. They removed as much of it as they could, but he would still need to undergo radiation and chemotherapy. He would have to stay at a rehab facility until he improved enough to go home. And he desperately wanted to go home.

During the next several weeks, I could not speak to my dad. He didn't want to talk on the phone. He wasn't well. He told me, "Chris, I'm sick. I have to go." That was so hard because I couldn't even tell him how much I was thinking of him, which made me feel so distant. He would allow my brothers to come visit, but he told them, "I am not ready to see your sister." I don't know if it was his pride or something else, but I think deep down inside, he didn't want his little girl to see how weak he had become. My dad was not a real phone-call kind of guy. He preferred to talk in person, but we had always been able to have quick talks, and to know he couldn't do that just killed me.

The surgery was the first of August. He continued to live at the rehab facility for several weeks after the surgery. The prognosis the doctors had given my brother Mike was that, best-case scenario, Dad would only have another six to twelve months. But this was a best-case scenario and depended on how well he did with the radiation and chemo. Dad didn't know this, and we struggled with how to tell him. How would we tell a man who was in the fight of his life that even if all went perfectly well, he still only had six to twelve months?

We all talked and eventually felt it was Dad's right to know the truth. Mike was there with him, and he broke the news. Dad's reaction was shock. "Ah, come on!" he said. I think it just slipped right through his ears and left, as there was never talk of that again.

Dad was finally released to home care, and with this came new and regained hope. We all put the time frame the doctors had given Dad out of our minds as well, as he seemed to rally us around the thought that this silly notion of six to twelve months was nonsense. He was able to walk short distances but still required the use of a walker. But he was home, and for him, this was all he needed.

He started taking my calls again, and he asked when I was going to come visit. I was so happy to hear this. I told him of course I would come right away. I made my flight plans for the following week. A couple of days with Dad would be wonderful. I didn't want to overstay my welcome and didn't want to overwhelm him. A few days would be just right.

I arrived on a Monday morning. When I walked into his home, Dad was all cleaned and shaven, sitting in his La-Z-Boy chair. He was thin, and the strands of hair he had left were combed to one side. He was wearing his usual shorts, clogs, and a Marine veterans T-shirt. He struggled to get up, and I told him just to sit, but he insisted and we went outside to his deck.

The day went by fast, and I tried to find things I could

do to help. The tumor and surgery had left him a different man. I could see in his eyes that he was trying to put on a brave face. But behind that was the fear, the worry, the reality.

The day was winding down. Earlier, Dad had kept saying he wanted to have dinner "al fresco." A man who enjoyed the spirit of an outdoor barbecue with family and friends, he would always say, "Tonight we dine al fresco." He was a great cook, and the meaning of sharing family and a good meal was priceless to him.

He asked if I would go pick up some Mexican food from his favorite place in town. And he gave me orders for exactly one chicken quesadilla with guacamole, extra sour cream, and three containers of pico de gallo. "Not that runny salsa stuff. Make sure it's the house-made pico de gallo." Dad had lived in various parts of Mexico, and to him, this would be great comfort food. We set the time for dinner around when the sun was setting: five thirty on the dot, not a minute later. His military days had made Dad very punctual, and there was no room for tardiness when it came to matters such as this. He went inside to nap, and I took off to pick up our dinner. I returned exactly at five fifteen sharp.

The warmth of the day had started to lighten, and a slight coolness in the air blew through. I set the table with the finest of paper plates and plasticware while Dad sat in his chair and gave me instructions on what to do. Once the table was set, he said that he'd like a cold beer with dinner and invited me to join him for one. So I went inside and got two cold Blue Moons out of the fridge.

Just as predicted, the sun was setting over the mountains of Tucson and the sky began to turn a deep-red and orange color. We ate our quesadillas and sipped on the cold beer. Dad loved a cold beer. Fighting cancer and a hard diagnosis was not going to take that away from him, and I didn't even bother trying to explain it. I just accepted it, and we both appreciated the moment together.

After dinner, we were having some light chitchat. His energy was fading, and the give-and-take of normal conversation was taking its toll. But the colors were still so beautiful, and I knew he was soaking it in. I thought about a nice story I could share with him. So I started to tell him about Milagro.

I told him the whole story. He was aware that I had a horse in my life from the Christmas cards I'd sent and the little thing or two I'd told him here or there. But he didn't know the real story from the beginning. I told Dad all about my Milagro. And when I finished the story, his eyes were suddenly free from the weight of his situation. He looked me straight in the eye and said, "You did good, Chris." I had spent my whole life loving horses, and Dad knew that this was where my journey had taken me. He was proud of me, not for saving Milagro but for being true to myself even when he doubted. Long ago, back in the barns of Germany, a seed had been planted, and here it was, still growing strong after all these years. In some strange way, I think sharing the story of Milagro with my dad, at that moment, let him know I was going to be OK. I think he knew he would be leaving soon and he worried about his kids, but something in the story of Milagro told him that I was able to find my way. He didn't need to worry about that anymore.

The next day, I packed up for the airport. Dad asked if I could come again, and I told him I would be back in a

Dad, San Carlos, Mexico

couple weeks. We hugged, and as I drove out of the driveway, I looked back and saw him sitting in his chair on the
patio. He'd told me that morning how good it was to see
me, and it was the first time since he'd been home that he
had "dined al fresco." I held that thought in my heart as
I drove to the airport. As I left Tucson that afternoon, I
had no idea that I would be back in a matter of days. And
there would be no more dinners on the patio with Dad.
I had no idea that things were going to shift, once again
for the worse.

Two days after getting home from Tucson, we got a
text from Mike. Dad was back in the hospital, and they
were recommending hospice. *Hospice?* I was just there
a few days earlier, and Dad had seemed completely onboard with his treatment plan. I had gone with him to

radiation, and we had talked about the chemo and the time frame for completion of the treatments. Both Mike and Tony were unable to go out to Tucson because of work. So Keith and I talked about it briefly, and it seemed the best thing was for me to turn around and drive back out there. He was about to be discharged from the hospital, and I wanted to be there to ensure whatever was happening was what he wanted. So I packed a few things, got in the car, and headed east.

I arrived in time to go over everything with the hospital staff. Dad didn't look the slightest bit surprised to see me back there. He was not ready to make any decisions about hospice yet, so we put that on hold until he could make a clear decision. It was raining, and as we got him home and into his La-Z-Boy chair, he was exhausted.

The following morning, I woke up early and left my hotel to go to his house. I wanted to have a chance to speak to him before everyone began to bustle about. I needed to have some privacy with him. I talked with him and then asked him straight up if hospice was something he wanted to consider. He closed his eyes for the longest time, suddenly opened them and looked at me, and said he didn't want to do any more of these treatments. He didn't want to go to the hospital anymore. He wanted to stay home and be cared for at home. He didn't want to fight anymore. He was waving his white flag. We both knew what this meant. In giving up the fight, he was accepting his fate. The time frame came back into play. But it didn't matter anymore. He was choosing. He said enough is enough. He wanted to have whatever time was left on the clock be on his terms.

I spent the next eight days in Tucson. We made the

necessary arrangements for hospice care. The nurse assigned to him reminded me so much of my grandmother Lillian. My dad's mother had flaming-red hair and pale skin, and always had a coffee can of red lipstick by the kitchen sink. The nurse looked much the same and also had a warm graciousness about her that reminded me of my Nana. I asked Dad if he thought the same, and he gave me half a laugh and said, "Yeah, she sure does."

The days melted into one another. Dad had sat down in his La-Z-Boy chair when he arrived home from his final journey to the hospital. And that was exactly where he stayed. The aide would come and bathe him as best she could. His catheter ran down his leg to the plastic bottle on the back of the chair. He had his small table where his reading glasses sat, along with a plastic cup and straw he had from the hospital. He was steadily drinking the replenishing fluids. I couldn't believe how thirsty he was.

He was sleeping almost all the time by now, living mostly in a state of rest, but if we spoke to him, he would open his eyes to respond. Other times, he seemed perfectly asleep and then suddenly would jerk and open his eyes and look around to see that I was there. In those eyes, he showed his fear, and his vulnerability. And once he caught sight of me, he would relax. I felt so good to be able to provide at least that simple comfort.

So much went on behind the scenes with the questions about, and management of, his care. But for Dad, things seemed very calm and quiet. On the eighth day, my brother Mike arrived to relieve me so that I could go home. I was exhausted, but I knew that each moment spent was priceless. And now that I was going home, I was almost certain these days were the last that I would spend with my dad. My daddy, it was all coming to an end.

Mike stayed another week, and then Dad's nurse gave us the news. He had declined so much that she told us, "It's just a matter of days." Tony and Cindy decided to drive out to Tucson. I planned to catch an early-morning flight the following day. We hoped that he could hold on long enough for us all to be there. The time frame was closing in.

I woke up at 4:00 a.m. and quickly took Roy for his morning walk. As the darkness of the morning hung over us, the moon and the stars shined down brightly. Roy moved slowly across the grass, and I watched him sniff for his perfect place. I had a lot of things tossing and turning in my head, and my stomach felt jittery. As we walked a bit farther, I suddenly had a feeling of relief. Something washed over me, and that internal voice spoke out and said, "You don't need to rush, or worry. You won't be flying anywhere today."

As Roy and I entered the house, I could not so much as put the leash away before my phone rang. It was Tony. I answered and heard his somber voice simply say, "He's gone."

I didn't fly out that morning. I decided to stay home and be comforted by my little family. Keith consoled me. No matter how much I'd prepared, I was never prepared. But I knew that little voice I'd heard tell me I didn't need to rush, or to worry, was my dad speaking to me. As fast as a spirit can travel, he came to me that morning after he passed and spoke those final words to me. And as I had always done throughout my whole life, I listened to my father.

Family Gathering

IT WAS ONLY A MATTER OF WEEKS before the Thanksgiving holiday was upon us. Mike had been able to get Dad's ashes, and we all planned to be together for the holiday. Then we would have a small family reception to honor our dad.

Tony and Cindy hosted the family Thanksgiving dinner. I made arrangements to pick up Mom and bring her to their house. She was so far into her state of dementia that we didn't know what to expect. And with the recent loss of our dad just a few weeks prior, we were all aware of how this could be another blow to the heart.

But Mom was full of surprises that day. Keith and I had bought her a pretty winter-white turtleneck with a sequined sweater to match. The ladies at the home had done her makeup, and she seemed to understand this was a day to celebrate. Mom had always hosted Thanksgiving. The way she was now was a far, far distance from the lady of Thanksgivings past.

The whole family and some close friends were at the house, close to twenty people, and Mom didn't seem bothered in the least with the chaos and craziness that was going on. Loud chatter with a mix of barking dogs, music, laughter, and voices mingling—she just seemed to take it all in. She sat in a chair at the bar in the kitchen and watched in wonder.

When the dinner was ready to be served, Cindy had us all gather in a circle and hold hands for the blessing. As we clasped our hands and bowed our heads, ready to hear someone's words of wisdom, Mom suddenly broke into what I can only describe as a song and a ramble. She rose

from left Tony, me, Mom, Mike on Thanksgiving Day

up her hands with those she held on to and proceeded to give the blessing. Not a word of it was intelligible, but it went on for quite some time, and as we all watched in awe, our faces broke into smiles of bewilderment. At one point, she paused, so I spoke out a swift "AMEN," to which she said, "Ta-da!!!!" And she put her hands down in a way that told us all she was done and it was time to eat. "Amen," we all said.

I sat next to her and watched as she fed herself, enjoyed a splash of wine, smiled, and lived in the moment. She had not a care in the world, and although she was so apparently absent, she was also so present. It was a beautiful gift.

Milagro's Struggle

I WAS GOING TO THE BARN regularly to see Milagro, and we had recently begun to ride again. After trying to find a western saddle that fit him just right, I finally gave in and decided to buy a dressage saddle. It fit his short back and small body perfectly. But I had never ridden English or dressage, so when we did start riding again, I felt like a beginner. And to Milagro, my lack of confidence was one more obstacle.

The plan to give him the summer off from riding, do ground work only, and let him muscle up came from good intentions. But I didn't know this horse as well as I thought I did. For most horses, the routine of riding, exercising, and connecting with their owners is a vital part of feeling whole. It was the same for Milagro, but for him, the lack thereof was interpreted as a danger zone, a place he did not want to enter into. It triggered the most profound instinct in him, and that was one of survival. In his world, where he had come from, lack of work meant lack of food as well as neglect, and it set off the fight-or-flight instinct all horses have. This horse had been there, and he knew how fast he could slip back into that devastating cycle. I had no idea it would trigger this in him. Not to mention when I came to the barn, I was carrying a lot of worry on my shoulders, which only added to his sense of uncertainty.

The past months had been full of anxiety, not only for my dad but also for my mom, Roy, and Keith's mom and dad. It was never ending. I would go to the barn to spend time with Milagro to try to escape—my own fight-or-flight. I was running to him to help me through my own fight for survival. I was a whole hot mess of anxiety, fear, and grief, waiting for the next shoe to fall. Poor Milagro—the more I leaned on him, the more he pulled away. He didn't recognize this person. The girl who had all the courage and hope back in Cabo had turned into a sad state of affairs. He needed me. He needed a strong and decisive person he could lean on. But I was too caught up in my own pain and angst to recognize it.

The issues that had started back in the summer were now only escalating. I found myself fearful of his unpredictability. I felt as he did. Who was this horse? Where was my confident, levelheaded, strong Milagro? Why was he acting this way? And so the vicious cycle that started as a small kindling began to burn between us. I just had no idea what to do.

Saying Goodbye

TWO WEEKS AFTER MY DAD PASSED and shortly before Thanksgiving, our dog, Roy, started his own descent. I couldn't believe the timing, although I knew each precious day with him was a gift. One afternoon, he just couldn't get comfortable. Each time he tried to lie down, he sat up quickly and started panting. He was in pain, and we couldn't tell what exactly was happening or where. I called the vet, talked to her, and asked, "Is it time?" The pain meds he was on could be increased, but to what avail? Her honesty had never failed me, so I trusted when she said, "I don't think it is off the mark to start having this conversation." We didn't want to end up with Roy in some sudden emergency situation. We wanted to allow him the peace and dignity he deserved. But here it was, two weeks after my dad's passing. We decided to up the pain meds for the short term and see how it went.

The increase in dosage did help, and within twenty-four hours, Roy was looking and acting more like himself. I would find myself watching him sleep and counting his breaths to look for signs of distress. But he had found a new plateau, and with that we heaved a sigh of relief. I knew it was short-term, and the conversation was now a daily part of our lives. But for now, he was eating well, enjoying his walks, and greeting his friends and neighbors with a smile and wag of the tail.

The Christmas season was hard. We went through our regular rituals of decorating a tree, buying presents, and going to Christmas parties. My heart was still heavy from losing my dad but also filled with worry and concern over Roy.

Christmas came and went, and we knew it was time to make arrangements to say goodbye to Roy. The few weeks that the pain meds had bought us were precious and unforgettable. But we couldn't hide in the comfort of denial. It was time. It was time for him to fly—and for us to say goodbye.

January 2, we woke up knowing this was the last day we would spend with our boy. He had been through so much with us. And for me, he had been every bit the rock I needed. He was my heart; he was my home. He encompassed everything, and I couldn't imagine living without him.

He had his breakfast with an extra serving of scrambled eggs and sausage. The morning was clear as a bell, and cool and crisp. We decided to walk him the extra distance today, to the coffee shop so he could see his dog friends and we could share a blueberry muffin together with him. It was amazing how much energy he had. We had been keeping his walks guarded and safe, but today he could sense we were not about that. We were about going for the moment. And he was so cheerful and energetic.

He slowed his pace on the way home, as I think the excitement had caught up with him. We got home and decided to lay a blanket down outside on the grass in the shade so he could enjoy the sounds of the morning. The birds chirped and the sun rose higher. I soaked up his dog breath and loved on his sweet, soft, furry head and ears. I could not believe that we were about to say goodbye.

The doctor from Graceful Departures showed up, and we all went inside. At that point, Keith took to his office and the back patio. He could not hold it together. And that was OK. As much as I had dreaded this, there was absolutely no other place I'd be at that moment in time. I was going to be there for him to the very end. There was comfort in knowing I could do that for Roy.

We all sat together on the large living room rug. Roy was brave and came right up to the doctor as if he knew why she was there. The pet psychic had told me a few months before—when she said she thought he would be sticking around through the holidays—that they see dying as a journey home. I think Roy saw the doctor as the one who was going to take him there.

Kitty came out to make an investigation herself. She leaned in and took a sniff of the little black box. She did this and then walked over to Roy and sniffed his nose. And then she, too, retreated to her safe place. Later I found her cuddled up at the top of her cat tree.

So then it was the three of us. After I said my final farewell, the good doctor slipped him the magic cocktail and he was gone. His body lay silent and still. And that's when the tears rolled from my eyes in big puddles faster than I had ever felt before. My heart sank to a dark and dreadful place, where it would stay for as long as it took to crawl back out. It physically hurt to breathe.

The doctor gave me as much time as I needed to collect myself. And then I helped her carry him on the cot to her vehicle. She promised to have his ashes to me within ten days, and also a clay print of his big ol' paw. My best friend was gone. My dad was gone. And my mother hinged on the same fate.

Moving Milagro

THE EL NIÑO WINTER that had been forecasted for that season was beginning to show its true colors. Milagro's stall was half-covered, but the rest of it was wet and muddy. The arenas were closed for days as we waited for enough sun to dry them out, and then *bam*, another storm would come rolling in. It was dangerous to even try to get him out of his stall to hand walk, as the mud was very slippery. So on my visits to see him, all I could do was offer him some treats and work on digging trenches to let the standing water run off. Poor Milagro—our first six months in the land of plenty had proven to be challenging in ways I couldn't have foreseen. He'd always been in a herd, and in Cabo, he had daily turnouts with the other horses for hours at a time. Here, he was always kept to himself in his pen or in an arena with me. I didn't see it then, but later I realized just how important this was for his sense of well-being. He missed the comfort and security of the herd.

After the New Year, I decided I couldn't take a winter like this. Milagro deserved better. So on the first weekend in January, the owner of a new barn not too far away came to fetch Milagro and take him to yet another new home.

Milagro settled into his new stall as best he could. It was a bit smaller in size, but fully covered and bedded in fresh shavings. I thought it was every horse's dream. And he would be dry and happy in this new place. He had neighbors, but here at this barn, there was wire to prevent the horses from biting each other. This also prevented them from nuzzling and sniffing each other in a meaningful social way. In Cabo, Milagro had been in a stall made of cinder blocks, so this didn't seem to be of concern to me. But in Cabo, he also was given ample time out in the paddock with the horses. Here, there was going to be none of that.

The long row of barns sat up somewhat on a flat carved out of the hillside. Below the barn sat a large arena, and more stalls of horses. Milagro called out towards the other horses at first. He paced and showed some nervousness, but this is all to be expected when a horse comes to a new home. I walked him around the grounds to let him get his bearings. He spooked and was jumpy in ways that made me nervous. He seemed amiss as to what was happening. I started to regret this decision and thought that too many changes in such a short time were not fair to him. But the rain was coming, and I would feel even worse leaving him in a stall open to the El Niño season. This new change would have to do, and we would have to work through it.

The weather continued to be erratic, and on rainy days, I came to at least get Milagro out of his stall for some hand walking. On other days, we were able to access the round pen for some real exercise. He was growing increasingly unpredictable, and I had no idea who this levelheaded horse had turned into. When walking past anything that made an unusual sound, or just a gust of wind, he would lunge forward or sometimes even rear up in fear. When turned out in the round pen, he snorted and pranced and ran with his eyes wide and his head held high, doing his best to get a look over the tall fence. Walking him into the round pen was difficult, and he would lunge in and out of the gate past me, practically knocking me over. It seemed the more I tried to let him have time to get the bucks and kicks out, the more agitated and nervous and fearful he became. Of what, though? What was this horse so afraid of? He had his meals on schedule and a safe, dry, and comfortable barn to live in. I was coming to the barn every other day or so. Was this the healthy version of Milagro that had lurked inside the unhealthy horse who had been through the ringer? What kind of training had he really had? Was the round pen a negative place for him, and was that the problem creating the fear? I looked high and low, and talked to as many people as I could. I wanted to know what on earth had gotten into him and how I was going to work through this.

These days were hard. There had been small issues and warning signs at the last barn, but it felt like suddenly Milagro and I were no longer working as a team. We were pulling away from each other, and I no longer trusted him. A large animal like this can do damage, and I constantly worried about him getting into trouble or me getting hurt. I began to dread going to the barn, and the time spent there was no longer in-the-moment. I was in my head all the time, trying to stay two steps ahead of his emotions and reactions.

We went out of town for a few days, and I made arrangements for Candy, the barn manager, to get Milagro out for a turnout. We were driving, and I texted her to see how things had gone that day. She told me that she had taken him from his stall and he'd bolted shortly after, trying to get away from her. She was worried, so she returned him to his stall, where he raced back and forth from one side to the other, tucking and spinning. She said, "Christie, it was the craziest thing. He was like a wild horse trying to flee in fear." I couldn't believe it. Candy had the best horse sense out there, so to have him act out in this way only added to my concern.

I talked to my vet, and she had just recently done his physical and seasonal shots. She told me there was nothing out of the ordinary medically with him. She was at a loss. One thing I could do was to enlist the help of a trainer. But what did we need training for? I knew how to care for him; I knew how to ride. But I didn't know how to work out this problem.

Candy at the barn recommended a young lady named Kaila. She had practically grown up at the barn and was now in her late twenties with a small family. Candy said she really knew her stuff and, if anything, she could give me some tips. So I gave Kaila a call, and we set up a time to meet.

Training

It felt like springtime, suddenly. The rains had stopped, and the place had finally gotten a chance to dry out. All the arenas were open. The grounds and walkways were dry again. It felt lighter, and there was a bit more ease at the barn. But Milagro and I had made no progress.

Kaila came to meet us on a Tuesday morning. She sat on the bench under the tree while she watched me groom Milagro. She listened as I told her all about his troubles and explained that I just had no idea why he was acting out this way. Yes, we had only been together for a few years, but back in Cabo, I felt that I really knew and understood Milagro. On the very first day I met him, I felt we were meant to be and trusted him immensely. Now I struggled to find that comfort once more.

She sat with her arms tucked and listened to me. She seemed so easy to talk to that I shared with her that the past few months had been hard for me in other ways, and that this issue with Milagro was really wearing me down. I told her about my dad dying in October and Roy passing just two months later. There was my mom, who had been sick for so long and was steadily heading downhill. I told her that it had been a very hard couple months.

Once Milagro was groomed, she said that we were not even going to tack up today. She wanted to observe us, and she asked me to take Milagro's lead and walk him in a certain direction.

So I did, and immediately he bounced his head and front legs in what could be described as a small rear. I looked at her with that "see, I told you so" face, and she just showed me a soft, non-expressive face. She walked over to us and took the lead, and she then walked Milagro in the same direction, and this time, he was very polite and happy to follow her. She led him to the hitching rail and tied him up, and then she turned to me and politely told me what was going on.

It seemed to her that I was approaching my horse with a lot of apprehension and looked like I was bracing for something to happen. My arm was long and stiff as if trying to lead a baby along a dangerous path. My shoulders were sinking forward, and my head was held back away from him as if I was trying to avoid him. Instead of walking forward, I was halfway facing him, which also sent a message of unease.

I listened to her and took to heart what she was telling me. In her very humble yet "it's really all you" attitude, she was basically telling me I was the problem. I was very relieved to know she saw a path for us to get back on the right track. But I felt so confused. How had I gotten so off-track? I'd never, ever felt uneasy about being around a horse. My confidence had always been almost a sense of blind faith. But I wasn't that person any longer. These past difficult months had been brought on by my behavior.

We continued the lesson, and for the next thirty minutes, we walked the property. I couldn't believe that after all these years, now in my forties, I was having a lesson on how to walk my horse on a lead. But we needed to take things back to this. Milagro had lost his leader. She had slipped between the cracks, and it was obvious now that she needed to crawl her way back out. If it took baby steps, then that's what it would have to be. Milagro had cast a light into my inner state of being, and the reflection was one of a person who existed in such an anxious and fearful state. I was fragile. I was bracing—bracing for one more loved one to go, bracing for the utter heartbreak I'd been dealt in just two short months. First losing my dad to an aggressive brain cancer, and then Roy's passing two months later—you bet your high horse I'd been bracing. The tides had been rough going, and I'd thrown myself into the ups and downs of all of it. I needed to walk away and get my steady gait again. I had to. Milagro would not have it any other way.

Kaila instructed me gently but firmly. She knew this had been difficult for me to absorb, but, as with horses, she didn't want to give me time to dive too far into it. What I needed most was to come out of this lesson on a high note. So we walked, she talked, and I took the baby steps necessary to begin turning us around. "Don't brace your arm," she would say. "Soften your shoulders. Carry the lead loosely, walk with a natural cadence. You are bracing again. That's good, very good! Don't let him rush. Back him up when he rushes forward like that." Over and over, we went through elementary moves, and by the end of it, Milagro had lowered his head in a sign of trust. He was licking his lips and taking deep breaths, all good signs that what we were doing was making him feel safe and relaxed.

Kaila left after we made plans to meet again the following week. We'd made great progress in just one lesson, but I needed more time with her. We both needed it. And Milagro, for the first time in months, walked slowly and calmly to his stall and showed me that side of him that I'd grown to know back in Cabo. His trusting eyes looked at me as I tried to tell him how sorry I was to have turned into such a mess. He looked at me as if he, too, was recognizing the person he knew not so long ago. And from that day forward, I knew that my horse needed me more than ever. He needed me to be strong and present. He had no understanding of the anguish I carried. When I brought that to the barn, all he read was fear and unsteadiness, and horses do not do well with those things. He had been picking that up from me and wondering what in the world we should be running from. I had been running long and hard. I'd been running from all the sadness and fear I had over losing my loved ones. I ran from the pain and sadness that welled up in my heart. I ran from reality, as it had been almost too much to bear.

That day was a huge turning point for me. Not only did I need to step up for Milagro, but I realized the all-too-important lesson of doing my best to stay in the moment, keeping my mind from being occupied by forces I had no control over. I needed to let all that worry go and focus on what was happening in front of me.

Milagro only knew how to exist in the present. And his ability to reflect my own inner turmoil back to me helped pull me off of a very dangerous path, one that I could have stayed on for a very long time.

After this recent revelation with Milagro, it was time for me to lay down my shield and to accept the things I had been running from. There would be more to come. Mom's decline was accelerating at a fast pace. She wasn't going to be with us much longer. I had spent too much time ducking and dodging the sorrow and the grief. And I had paid a price. I knew I needed to learn to grieve and go on. It just had to be.

If it hadn't been for Milagro, though, I don't know how long I would have stumbled around in this space. If it wasn't for his ability to shine a mirror on my internal emotional state, it may have gone on for much, much longer. My friend was there to remind me of the beauty in choice. I could choose to continue living in that state or to work on moving past it. And I would do just about anything for Milagro. The choice was made. I would do it for the both of us.

It was March now, and Milagro and I had made leaps and bounds with our training sessions with Kaila. We quickly moved from the ground work, which had been so vital, to riding lessons. Our new dressage saddle gave us an opportunity to learn something new together. So with Kaila's help, we worked on the basics. Our trust in each other was strong once again.

Full Circle

KEITH AND I HAD MADE A BIG DECISION during this time as well. Our house in Park City had tenants, but they decided to buy a home. This meant that it would be vacant sometime in June. We had the choice of either renting our home to another tenant and staying in San Diego for another year or finally making our way home.

It had been a long, amazing, and full five years. Our time in San Diego had been well spent. Keith's dad had gone through his hip surgery. We had spent a lot of time helping them get their home better suited for aging folks. Keith's mom had suffered from strokes and also had signs of dementia. We had tried to help get his mom into a home or help his dad get an aide for her at home. But eventually they got to a point where they felt stable in their home, and with Bob's new hip, he had a renewed level of confidence about their current living situation. It appeared our help was no longer needed.

In March, we also received news that my mom was going to be put on hospice. Her doctor made the painstaking recommendation after a recent checkup with her. He had known my mom for several years now. And as a board member of the Department of Alzheimer's and Dementia of Sharp Rees-Stealy Medical Group, he recognized the telltale signs of a woman who was reaching the end.

My brothers and I agreed that this was the right step for her. With the help of her counselor, we were able to move her to a skilled nursing home that could offer all the care she would need. I hated to see her move from the ladies' home she had grown to know. It really felt like a home there, not a sterile hospital. But they were not equipped for hospice care. It was the only choice.

This would be the final place for Mom. We knew that. She had been through two different homes and had always taken the change with a bit of an adventurous spirit. They say those with Alzheimer's don't do well with change, but that was not the case with my mom. She had made both of her previous moves into a grand adventure. I often wondered what she thought as she experienced these changes. But it was evident to us in the way she responded to her new surroundings that the road we call life was still alive. Bless her heart. Her positive attitude made it so we could proceed without such agony.

Keith and I talked, and I knew that moving back to Park City meant I would not see my mom as much as I had been able to. Luckily we had been there to go through these big changes with her. But she would be in the caring hands of our family who lived in San Diego: my brother Tony and his wife, Cindy, as well as Mom's grandkids and great-grandkids. And I would visit as much as I could. It had been five years, and we were ready to go home after living abroad and then moving back to San Diego. The last year had been full of ups and downs. The timing could not have been better, as so much had happened in that one short year. How amazing it had been that it worked out that way. But with Keith's parents stable and my mom settled into her new home, it was time we made our way back to the home we loved and had always known we would return to.

The skilled nursing facility just so happened to be a ten-minute drive from Milagro's new barn. So a few months after moving him, she was once again only a short distance away. I was again able to have an easy visit with her after my riding at the barn, as they were so close to each other once more. My last few months in San Diego had finally reached a place of peace and contentment. The worry and fear peeled away, and I relished this newfound sense of self.

I cherished each visit with Mom in those final months before we moved back to Utah. Knowing that things would change for her any day gave me a deep appreciation of those moments we had together. It was a bittersweet time. A few days a week, I'd go out and ride Milagro at the barn and then head over in my dirty breeches and riding boots to say hi to Mom. I was always in a lifted mood after spending time at the barn with Milagro, and it helped to build me up so that seeing her in that state didn't bring me down. The lift I carried from the barn to the nursing home was vital to my emotional strength.

It was painful. It felt uncomfortable to be with her and not know what to say. There was not much of a light inside her any longer. It was hard to sit in that uncomfortable space with the ghost of the woman I once knew. But I knew what I was capable of, and so with my armor of breeches, dusty boots, and shirt wiped in horse sweat, I trotted into the nursing home with courage and a brave face.

At this point, all my mom could read or understand anymore was my facial expression. If I was bright-eyed and bushy-tailed, she would light up, and I found ways to be comfortable in that most uncomfortable of places. She would hold my hand or stroke my hair and look deep into my eyes. Peeling back the layers of the cobwebs that clogged her memory, she tried so hard to make that connection. And sometimes her eyes would fill with tears. She'd smile, and the tears would roll down her cheeks as if that spark ignited deep inside her mind, and I would see my mom. If only a shimmer of her shined through before the darkness crept back in, those beautiful shimmers gave me conviction that she was still there. Her expression would come alive, and in that split second, it was like, "hello, stranger." And then off into the shadows she would go.

I usually stayed for twenty or thirty minutes, long enough to keep my armor intact, as the more time I stayed, the harder it became to stay strong. I knew I needed to leave on a high note, so when I felt that sadness begin to well up in me, I'd gather up my things and give her a quick kiss on the cheek. Then I would say in a strong and upbeat voice, "OK, Mom, I'm leaving now, but I will see you tomorrow"—a little white lie, as it would not be tomorrow that I would see her but perhaps days later. But Mom had taught me long ago that little white lies were acceptable as long as no one was hurt, that sometimes little white lies were needed so as not to cause pain or worry. My exit phrase was one she found comfort in, and she would give me a look of approval. And so it went.

Keith and I had packed up the house, and it was ready for the movers to come and take our things to Utah. We would be driving the two vehicles out, just as we'd done nine years prior. This time, we would travel that road without Roy. I'd hoped that he would stay strong and healthy enough to make it back to the mountains he loved so much.

We were also leaving behind our family and friends once again. I had enjoyed being so close to everyone for that short period of time. But the mountains were calling us home. It was time for us to go back to our first love, our first home, the house we had spent our first years of marriage in. So much had changed, more than I could put into words.

Arrangements had been made, and Milagro would be traveling to Utah with a proper horse transportation company, the same company that had been hired to move the great Triple Crown winner American Pharoah—no doubt this company would treat him with the best care I could hope for. It was not going to be anything like his eight-day adventure from Cabo to San Diego, but it was an important move nonetheless, and I took every precaution to ensure his comfort and safety.

We arrived in Park City the middle of May. After driving for two days with a stopover in Arizona, we finally rolled into town. The weather was cool and wet. The mountains still held their snow from the winter, but the springtime rains had moved in. Clouds topped the mountains, and the air was so fresh and welcoming.

We got a room at a nice pet-friendly hotel for the night. Kitty was traveling with us, and we needed a place to rest before meeting the movers the following morning. Our hotel room had a fireplace and a view of the snow-capped ski runs. It was a perfect welcoming for us, and we relished in the excitement of being back. Not just for a doctor appointment, or a visit—we were finally coming home to stay.

The following morning, we had a hearty breakfast at the hotel. We gathered up our things, and Kitty as well, and headed over to the house. The movers had texted and were only twenty minutes away.

The day went by quickly. The movers unloaded all our things and took them to their respective rooms. It was so nice to see our furniture fill up our house once again. Kitty ran around, sniffing all the different rooms taking in the sights and smells.

We spent the day getting the essentials in order. I unpacked some clothes and our toiletries. We made a trip to the grocery store to stock up on the basics. And by the end of the day, we were exhausted. Such excitement surrounded this day. The whole move to Mexico had been such an experience, and the final year in San Diego had been hard and challenging in ways I could not have foreseen. It had been a whirlwind, and I was happy and proud to have made the round trip and be back again.

Milagro spent an extra week in San Diego before the transport company could pick him up. It wasn't every day a horse was moving from San Diego to Park City, so to ensure he was on the rig only as long as deemed necessary, we needed to wait for them to have enough horses going out in that direction.

Candy at the barn was keeping in touch. The new Milagro who had calmed and settled himself after our troubled time was now no worry for her. She was giving him daily turnouts and keeping a watchful eye on him. When the day arrived for the transport company to collect him, she met the drivers and made sure all things went according to plan on that end. I was in Park City, busy unpacking our home and anxiously waiting for my boy to arrive. But there would be no quarantine or stressful tests this time around. He would be loaded in San Diego and make it to Park City the following afternoon.

The barn where I had chosen to keep Milagro was a

short drive from our house. I had driven past this barn too many times to count in the many years we lived in Utah. I would always watch the horses as they milled about in the pastures or watch riders go over jumps and through the fields. It was a very nice-looking place with a couple different barns and arenas, and a long driveway lined with trees that bloomed a beautiful white in spring. It had always appeared to be nothing short of a tightly run and well-cared-for barn. A small sign with the name of the stable and a short description, offering boarding and training, hung on the entrance to the driveway.

Months earlier, when Keith and I had been in Park City in February, we had taken a tour of this place with the owner, Jay. We met him one cold and snowy morning, and he showed us around. Jay had explained that the horses go out to pasture each day, all day. They have their break-fast and dinner in their stalls but are turned out to spend the day socializing, grazing, and just being horses. I had never had any of my horses in a pasture like that before.

But this concept sounded like a perfect way for Mi-lagro to spend his days. Deep down inside, I knew he missed being in a herd. He had always been kept with other horses in Cabo, spending most of his life ranging on the sand and desert of the Baja. Even at Saul's place, he was turned out for hours at a time each day with the other horses. Moving him to San Diego and keeping him compartmentalized in the 24 x 24 corrals was not a good feeling for him. He did well enough, but I could tell by the way he acted that he missed this very important aspect of life. In his eyes, I could see the yearning for that secu-rity and companionship.

I told Jay we would be moving our horse out in late

May, so he put us on his calendar. No paperwork was required, he just asked for half a month's board to hold a stall for us. And with that, he shook our hands and said, "See ya in the spring."

I had been in touch with him several times, and he knew Milagro would be arriving by transport soon. I'd gone out and chosen Milagro's stall. It just so happened that a corner stall next to the big roll-up doors would be available by the time he arrived. Milagro would get to enjoy a beautiful view of the gardens as well as the sunrise that leaked into the barn in the early morning. It was perfect.

I got word from Candy in the afternoon on the last day of May that Milagro had been loaded and was on his way. She told me he was in good spirits and was happy and calm when leaving the ranch. Candy wished us well and asked me to let her know when he made it to Utah. I thanked her for everything. Each step in this journey had been an important one, and I appreciated my time with them and all the help and care they had offered. I had my fingers crossed that our good luck in finding caring people would continue to Utah.

I went to bed that night with all the excitement of a little girl on Christmas Eve. The trip Milagro had taken to California had so much stress leading up to it. It was a time of such concern and uncertainty. This trip was truly one of going home. It was the victory lap, so to speak. The dream of taking this horse back to God's country was finally coming true. We had been through a lot, but we didn't lose sight of the dream. It was still alive and well. And tomorrow I would wake up and he would be here with us.

Milagro was to arrive in the afternoon, around three o'clock. I drove out to the barn. After a wait of an hour or more, the truck pulled up. I hadn't seen the truck, since Candy had loaded him in California. This was quite the horse transportation rig. The horses had stalls inside the trailer where they could move about safely. The door to the trailer was in the middle of the rig so they could lead them up and out without disturbing the other horses.

The two drivers came out and opened the large door, which created a ramp. The wooden ramp was lowered. Each driver had a lead rope attached to Milagro's halter to keep him from going off either side as they unloaded my precious cargo. I greeted him with a sigh of relief and a big "hello, buddy." He looked so good that it seemed the hours spent on his final leg of the journey had been a breeze. I was so relieved.

I took him over to his stall. Clean shavings lined the stall, and there was a fresh flake of alfalfa, which he began to nibble on. The other horses had been brought in from the field by that time, and some of them stuck their heads out of their stalls to see who this newcomer was. Milagro walked with his head low and his gait quiet.

I stayed for a while and watched to make sure he seemed comfortable and settled. I knew he was tired, so now that he was safe and sound in his new home, I bid him farewell. I would be out to see him in the morning. I gave him a big hug around his neck and a kiss on his muzzle. I had happy tears once more. Many happy tears had been shed along the way, and today was the end of the road.

Milagro's arrival in Utah

A Place Called Home

THE FOLLOWING MORNING, I awoke early with anticipation and excitement. Keith and I had a quick breakfast. He knew I had other things on my mind, so he was happy to see me shuffle out the door equipped with a bag of carrots and coffee in hand.

I arrived at the barn before the morning turnout. There wasn't anyone around, and I was happy to have some quiet time with Milagro. I walked into the barn, where his stall was at the end of the row. Some of the horses poked their heads out to see if perhaps I was

Miguel, the gentleman who led them to the field each day. When they didn't recognize me, they went back to eating their breakfast.

As I got closer to Milagro's stall, I heard the familiar whinny. For such a small horse, he had a strong and deep whinny. I reached in and patted him on the neck and gave him a carrot. The sun was streaming in through the metal slats. The cool air of the night was holding tight as the beginning of a new day filtered in. The sunlight captured tiny particles in the air, and Milagro glowed in specks of tiny gold glitter. And for a moment, I just enjoyed the beauty of this magical setting.

The view from his stall was picture-perfect. Looking east towards the large garden area were loads of blooming flowers that were working hard to capture the sun in the short growing season here in the mountains: gladiolas, giant iris, and daffodils, all in a kaleidoscope of color. A white picket fence framed the garden, with a green pasture beyond that reached as far as the eye can see. Large maple trees rested against the fence, where birds had made their nests. The chorus of chirps and song created a lovely soundtrack. And the air, the air was so fragrant and fresh. It swept my mind clear of any remnants of stress or worry.

To the far left of Milagro's stall was the farmhouse where Jay and his family lived. Opera music funneled from the house as his wife set out to tend to her garden, their small Springer Spaniel barking with delight and following diligently at her heels.

This was the kind of place I had always dreamed of as a child. I had a fascination with farms and barns. Real barns. Red-and-white barns filled with stalls. Beautiful rooms of wood with fresh pine shavings where pretty horses slept. I'd never been so lucky as to have a real barn while growing up. This place was just what I had always imagined. And now, here we were. Me and my horse.

This perfect red-and-white barn was nothing short of what a champion would expect. Although Milagro had no ribbons or trophies, he had won the greatest competition of all: survival. Now in this sanctuary so far from his old home, he had peace—the kind of peace that comes with a small barn full of other champions. And by the look on his face, he felt like he belonged. This horse knew that he was special and that at one point in his life, things weren't always so good for him. But now he claimed his spot proudly, with grace and ease amongst the others. He'd earned his place at the table, and this small yet special place in the mountains outside Park City was just about the best we could have imagined.

I put on his halter and led him out towards the grooming barn. By now, a few others had arrived, and I made introductions. Most of the horses here were ridden for show in one discipline or another. There were also several who were pleasure horses, or retired. There were two trainers, and one was also the barn manager. Both were very experienced with horses, and we were lucky to have them. Once again, we were in good hands.

We got into the grooming barn, and it was a bit overwhelming for me at first. I'd never been in such close quarters with other riders. In the grooming barn, there were eight grooming stalls lined up next to each other, with a row of lockers on the opposite side. A small office area with a viewing window to the indoor arena completed the building. It was similar to what I had ridden in as a very small child in Germany. It had been ages since I was anywhere near a barn with amenities such as this.

Milagro wasn't fazed at all by the setup of our new place, and his confidence and level of comfort helped me stay collected. It was our first day at a new school, so to speak, and just as always, having my steady best friend by my side helped me quickly get my bearings. In time, we saddled up and soon were riding in the big arena outside. By now, the other riders were on to something else, so we had the place to ourselves. We walked in circles, taking it all in, the views of the mountains and the acres of ever-green pastures. Cows milled about in the fields—huge cows bigger than Milagro. So much was in bloom. The trees hugged the railing of the arena, white with fragrant flowers. The crystal-clear sky covered us in a canopy of blue, and the sunshine leapt down to warm my cheeks.

Milagro wasn't allowed to go into the field for several days after arriving. He stayed in a smaller grazing area so that he could get acclimated, and slowly he was allowed more grazing time. With the fresh grass of spring, we had to be careful not to let him overdo it. But finally he was let out with the other geldings.

The field made him so happy. I could see how much this time of socialization meant to Milagro, and all the other horses as well. It was a calculated risk to let him out to play, but I also knew Milagro was a smart horse. These boarding-school horses were not familiar with the body language of their new Mexican schoolmate, and they responded accordingly. I had high hopes that Milagro would learn more of their language and not rely so much on his old ways. And he did.

Milagro's time in the field showed me his depth of courage. One of the smallest horses out there, he had the ability to hold his own. He spoke a language of confidence, and at the end of the day, when all the horses were anxious to get inside for their hay and grain, Milagro stood his ground to be one of the first. As Jay once said, "That horse has got some guts." After the fun and leisure time with the others, what mattered most to him was his sense of survival. And if it meant he would have to throw it down, so be it. The other horses seemed to understand. It was an essential part of life for Milagro.

Our first summer was such a beautiful time with all the new things we discovered, so far from the hardship of the longest summer. Running through the fields, flushing ducks from the ponds and marmots from the hills. Long, warm, and dry days that were never too hot for riding. Gorgeous blue skies with green fields leading to the base of Mt. Timpanogos. The tops of the mountains still white with the winter snow were like a scene out of Switzerland.

We made friends with the others at the barn. I got to know the ladies, and Milagro spent his days making friends and playing with the big boys in the field. I loved hearing stories of him out playing with the others. It was as if he was making up for lost time. He'd had a hard life, so much of it spent in neglect, tied up and waiting out the day in the heat of the Baja sun. He hadn't had time to explore his nature and to be happy, or to just be a horse. He had such a playful nature, and it warmed my heart to no end to know he was able to be free—free to play and graze to his heart's content. It gave me a great sense of satisfaction knowing that we had found our way to a

Field of Dreams

new beginning. Belonging to such a unique place was a priceless gift to us both. Without Milagro, I would never have been able to experience this dream. Every visit, every ride, every carrot. It came with a deep appreciation for this gift, something I never took for granted.

This peaceful place not only became our home but also was where Milagro finally laid down some roots and truly blossomed. Through days of exercise with the others in the field and our steady riding routine, his body transformed. The guidance of our new trainer, Oscar, continued our progress in the saddle, and Milagro's customized diet gave him what he needed for that final push to a beautiful state of health and recovery. It was as if he had turned back the clock and he had gained not only a new body but also a new perspective on life. It gave him hope.

Milagro and Me riding in the fall

Acceptance

ALL ALONG THE WAY, my health had been holding steady. The ups and downs with stressful times had left me exhausted and my mind fuzzy. The odd sensations and pains would come back. But with some rest, I was always able to bounce back. Muscle weakness or extreme fatigue, they always came and went. I learned to avoid the heat. And I began to listen to my body. It had a way of speaking to me, and when it needed attention, I learned not to dismiss its message. It was all a big learning curve, but after a few years, I wasn't so distracted by these things. It became part of the fabric of my life.

It had been three years since I'd first starting seeing Dr. Peters. The worry and what-ifs had taken a comfortable back seat to the main event of living my life as I saw fit. And, even though I still had my challenges, being out of the constant heat of Mexico and even Southern California was a huge improvement for me. The tests over the past three years had not shown any further decline. I seemed to be holding my own and found a place of acceptance.

I had an appointment with Dr. Peters in July. We went through the usual, and he ordered a new MRI to see if I'd had any new damage to my brain. As always, he said, "Just keep doing what you're doing." He gave me the thumbs-up on the way out the door. I was learning that MS was not so easy to put a finger on. I began to just be thankful that I wasn't getting any worse, and each visit, I felt like this might be my new normal. He didn't tell me that I was out of the woods. But he did give me confidence by telling me to "keep doing what you're doing."

My MRI came back good, as far as any further MS damage was concerned. But I had a new issue to deal with that had not been discovered previously, one that led me to a vascular neurologist, and more tests, new worries, and a new level of discontent. It was discovered that the right side of my main cerebral artery in my brain was damaged. It looked like a dry riverbed, with no blood flowing through it compared to the healthy left side. But my body, at some point, maybe even before birth, had grown new tiny blood vessels to make up for the big river being shut off. Now they were trying to figure out why. Had I had a stroke? A brain trauma? What were they to do about this? Did it leave me susceptible to a stroke? Or worse? To even further complicate things, none of this explained any of my MS symptoms. It was all so frustrating.

The vascular neurologist took my tests to a conference with other vascular neurologists from around the country. She shared my scans with the other doctors, as it seemed this was not something they saw every day. And after hearing some background about my current state of health, they collectively agreed that this was not something they could put their fingers on. There was no evidence that screamed out that I needed treatment or surgery to address the problem. After all this, there was really nothing they could tell me except to take a baby aspirin each day and to stay in touch. Watch for signs of weakness on my left side. And go on as I'd been doing.

All of this on top of the years of waiting and wondering about MS led me to one conclusion. I'd had just about as many tests as one could imagine, dealing with my head, and nothing showed any conclusive evidence pointing in any one direction. I was happy to have been in such great hands. And really, the doctors who had been looking after me were at the top of their game. But I needed a break. Unless something changed, I needed to take a hiatus from all the testing and let life take its course.

Peace for Mom

FALL WAS KNOCKING ON THE DOOR, and the leaves on the trees were beginning to change. Keith and I had made a short trip back to San Diego to see family in September. I visited with Mom, and she looked as thin and frail as ever. The visit had gone well, but it was the first time I noticed her crying so much. For most of that visit, she held my face and just wept. She had never been so emotional, and I wondered what she was thinking about that was upsetting her. But as much as I wished I could ask her, I knew that was not an option. So instead I sat with her and let her get it out. I just focused on loving her.

We left the nursing home, and I told Keith something was really different with her. The shimmer of light that used to shine through was completely gone now. I had never stopped praying for her to pass, as we all knew her life had no dignity, no joy. But now I felt an even deeper sense of urgency. Please, let her go.

Back in Park City, I was busy embracing my first true fall in five years. It was the season I loved more than any other, and I wanted to bask in its beauty. My health issues were set aside, and it took little effort to embrace this beautiful season.

Keith was an early riser, and as usual, he was up before me. He made his coffee, turned on the morning news, and then took a look at his cell phone. My brother had tried to call him at five o'clock that morning. He looked at my phone and saw my brother's number pop up with an alert and a voicemail.

Keith knew what this meant. But instead of waking

me, he let me sleep. After I'd gotten up and done some morning stretching, I came downstairs. He came up and hugged me with a deep warm hug, and I looked in his eyes and saw them fill with tears. Then he said, "Tony called this morning." And I knew what that meant. I didn't even have to hear the words from my brother's voice. My mom was gone.

We held each other for the longest time, and he listened as I softly cried. No matter the situation with Mom's health and the fact that we had all prayed for her to pass on to heaven, the finality of it was a blow.

I waited a few minutes to call my brother. When I did, he answered the phone and said, "Hey, sis," and went on to tell me that Mom had passed away in her sleep that night. She'd been found by the staff, and without so much as a whisper, she slipped away. By the light of a full moon, our mother put on her dancing shoes one final time and danced her way out of there. In the end, she had gotten her wish. She had always told me, "I hope when my time comes, I die in my sleep." And that's exactly how it happened. She'd been on hospice, so we thought we would get some inkling that she was getting very close. But that's not how things turned out, and I was relieved that not only did she have one final say about her life, but that our prayers had finally been answered.

Coming Home

IT WAS SUCH A BEAUTIFUL DAY. Keith and I took a walk to get some coffee and clear our minds. The air was so crisp and cool. The mountaintops where turning gold and red as the trees began to change color. The tall green grass of the summer was now a warm hue of earthy tones that only fall can bring.

My heart was heavy, but I was also relieved. Mom had waited long enough. She was the last of her family, and I could only imagine the reunion they were all having at her arrival.

After our walk, I told Keith I knew what I needed to do. I needed some time at the barn. I dressed, gathered up the usual bundle of carrots, and set out.

As I drove out on the quiet highway, passing the lake on one side and the ski lifts on the other, my heart ached and I did my best to hold back the tears. A whole lot had happened in these past several years. There had been so much change and so much loss.

As I pulled into the barn, the familiar sight of the horses frolicking in the field made me smile. I parked, went to my locker to get Milagro's leather halter, and headed out to round him up. And as I marched out into the field on that beautiful fall day, I noticed a change in me. I noticed that the heaviness I had carried through many of those challenges, and losses, in the past couple years had diminished. I felt lighter and stronger than ever. My mom had passed just hours ago, but I was now carrying a sense of peace.

Milagro saw me in the distance, and for some reason that day, he made a beeline for me, his gaze staring me straight in the eye as he trotted over grassy mounds until he reached me. He then came up and nuzzled my pockets. He knew there was a carrot waiting for him, but it also felt like a nudge, or a hug, of affection. We stood in the open field as he chewed his carrot, and I took a deep breath and looked around at all the beauty we had before us. And rather than wanting to lean on him for strength, and collapse into him as I had done so often in the past, instead I felt calm and assured. I gathered the lead rope and said, "Come on, buddy." And then I led him confidently to the barn.

We spent some extra time grooming, and I gave him some more carrots. His keen eye on me as I walked back and forth to my locker, he let out a deep, small whinny as if to keep my attention. This was a day just as any other for him. He always watched me carefully, and each time I looked into that sweet face, I felt better. We saddled up and made our way to the field. The girls were having a lesson in the arena, and the field seemed like a place we could find some space. I loved to ride spontaneously sometimes. Wind in our hair. No schooling, no plan. Just let it happen. Milagro loved riding in the field too, because he got to be close to the mares. This was their field, after all.

As we rode around, I noticed how quiet it was. So much tranquility, so much beauty. In the distance, I could see the big bay horses, Milagro's friends, clearing jumps. What a beautiful thing to watch their riders guide them around the arena in style. The neighbor's horses in the field next to us were leaning over the fence, curious to make our acquaintance. All the little things that were going on in this moment brought me such a sense of belonging.

Milagro and I rode in the field awhile longer. We

trotted this way and that, making figure eights and then stopping to catch our breath. As we sat soaking up the sun, I heard a buzzing sound coming from afar. It was an airplane that had come over the ridge, heading south. It was flying in our direction, and as it flew, it left a great-big white vapor trail above us. From one point to another, it covered the entire valley. As we stood and watched the plane disappear into the distance, I felt my mom's presence. She was there with us in that field of tranquility and peace. Her presence resonated in me. It was as if the plane was there to sprinkle a dose of her spirit around us. She was there to whisper to me, "You have all you'll ever need in the chambers of your heart."

And she was right. I had come to know this truth in the past years, from a painful divorce and the death of my first husband to starting over and finding my way in a new home in Utah. Then being uprooted again to start over in Mexico. Facing a devastating diagnosis that has no cure, the passing of my father, and losing Roy quickly after. All while dealing with the slow and painful decline of my mom, and her final passing. These past years had a way of knocking me down over and over again. But what I had learned was, no matter what I faced, where I lived, or how uncertain the future may be, if I kept my heart open, I would find my way. There are miracles out there that can happen. I just had to open my heart and believe in them.

And the old scars I carried from my childhood could eventually be healed. Life is not lived in a vacuum; change is inevitable. I vowed to never underestimate the power of change and the transformation it can bring.

Milagro and I watched the plane fly off in the distance. I gave him a loud click and a kiss, and he broke

into a canter across the field. We chased the plane until it disappeared behind the tall Timpanogos Mountains. And as I watched it disappear into the distance, I knew Mom and I had both found our way home.

The coming years brought Milagro and me even closer. And we grew to know those at the barn as well, and in time, people began to understand us. It was not a union based on competition or shows or ribbons, but one based on trust and friendship. A friendship that had begun as a beautiful meeting of two souls who needed each other. A friendship that had faced its share of challenges, always stepping up for one another and never forsaking the undeniable bond we shared. Milagro grew to become part of me. And his deep capacity to trust and forgive allowed him to love me too. Whatever secrets he had about his long life of hardship, he kept to himself.

So the young foal who had been born all those years ago during a night of storm and uncertainty was now here in this small mountain town. The little red gelding with the fishhook blaze had come so far. But like the colt who stood strong on the night of his birth, with a hurricane looming, he never lost his sense of self. His courage and resilience had endured. And like his forefathers, he had traveled a great distance to find his place, where he was meant to be, meant to start anew. He was part of our family now, and he would never have to worry again. Now he was amongst the strength and stature of other accomplished horses, and kind and caring people. In the beauty and serenity of the mountains of Utah, Milagro had finally found his place. He, too, had found home.

About the Author

GROWING UP IN A MILITARY FAMILY, and one of divorce and change, challenged Christie Bonham to find what she needed to root herself. Her love and passion for horses began at an early age. She spent her youth in 4-H and on her family's small ranch in the hills of California, which fostered her lifelong passion for all animals. Christie is an advocate for animal rescue and rehabilitation. She has invented and patented pet products as well as owned and operated a pet boutique and a pet-sitting business. She worked for many years as a professional in the legal field, which ignited her interest in writing as she spent days poring over legal briefs. She currently lives in Park City, Utah, with her husband, Keith, and their rescue pets, Mancha and Milagro.

Made in the USA
San Bernardino,
CA